SEVEN STAGES TO BECOMING
A SAVVY DIGITAL INVESTOR

TAMING CRYPTO

YOUR BEGINNER'S GUIDE TO NAVIGATING THE WILD WEST OF CRYPTO

BY MARYL GLADSTONE

DEDICATION

This book is dedicated to the millions of digital immigrants who, like myself, have found themselves frustrated and foggy about how to forge ahead through the maze of techie jargon, conflicting narratives, erratic economic conditions, and utter confusion when it comes to the current and future digital revolution that is blockchain and cryptocurrencies.

I was there . . . I feel you!

Maryl Gladstone

Published by Joyful Life Publishing, Imprint of Oro One Holdings, LLC

www.tamingcryptobook.com
www.marylgladstone.com

All rights reserved. No part of this book may be reproduced in any form by any electronic or mechanical means (including photocopying, recording, or information storage and retrieval) without permission in writing from the publisher.

For more information and bulk sales, please email hello@marylgladstone.com

©2023 by Maryl Gladstone
LIBRARY OF CONGRESS CATALOGING-IN-PUBLICATION DATA

Gladstone, Maryl
Taming Crypto: Seven Stages To Becoming A Savvy Digital Investor
Your Beginner's Guide to Navigating the Wild West of Crypto

Resources: tamingcryptobook.com/resources

ISBN (hardback) 978-0-9600013-2-3
ISBN (paperback) 978-0-9600013-0-9
LCCN #: 2023920392
Gladstone-Petreccia, Maryl

Editor: Richard Willett
Contributors: The Diotima Team including Torund Bryhn and Zachary Houghton, Lisa Duncan, Heidi Stangeland

Printed in the USA by IngramSpark and KDP.

DISCLAIMER

Aside from my work as an author, I spend my days investigating and identifying sound ways to invest, including within the new, decentralized digital asset and cryptocurrency economy. Considering that anyone who's been in the industry for more than four years is fondly referred to as an OG (original gangster), another way to say crypto "old timer", I am definitely a crypto late bloomer. I was drawn to blockchain and crypto by deep curiosity and, I admit, some FOMO. I searched for trustworthy sources that could teach me the do's and don'ts of this very foreign world. It soon became blatantly clear that finding information that I could actually digest and not feel like I was drinking from a fire hose wasn't so easy.

This book is my attempt at reconciling the micro and macroeconomic changes that technologies have now made globally pervasive so that, when it comes to our finances, rather than being gamblers making high-risk investment bets that will cost us, we can instead develop into becoming savvier speculators and investors in this DeFi (decentralized finance) economy. For that, you'll need to begin with some basic concepts before leaping into a more complex discourse about the world of cryptocurrencies.

This book is neither financial advice nor a financial directive telling you what to buy or how to invest. *Taming Crypto* is a beginner's guide that uses a tall tale filled with metaphors and sprinkles of philosophy to introduce this new digital world to those who might have some level of FOMO (fear of missing out) and who also love the Wild West (like I do). In this book, a family called the FOMOs steps into a journey chock full of adventures and misadventures, learning those lessons that will support them to realizing their dream of creating a new future on the untamed frontier. As someone new to crypto and blockchain, you'll have a parallel journey of your own into the world of cryptocurrencies and the decentralized, blockchain-based economy.

CONTENTS

INTRODUCTION: The Raw Truth: I Felt Really Lost   17

Why Taming Crypto?   21
So, Where Should You Start Reading?   26
Crypto Newbies, Start Here   26
So, Are You Ready to Get Wild?   32

PART ONE: The Story of the FOMOs   35

Introducing Centralized City   37
Meet the FOMOs   39
The Flood That Changed It All   47
PREP STAGE: Freddie's Plan   54
STAGE ONE: Get Ready: Mindset, Money, and Mapping   56
Now, For A Commercial Break
Back from the Break: Time to Meet Maverick   63
STEP TWO: Shopping for Assets   75
STAGE THREE: Perils of the Journey   82
STAGE FOUR: Get the Soft Wallet   84
STAGE FIVE: Time to Trade   100
STAGE SIX: Don't Get Misdirected!   106
STEP SEVEN: Safe at Home   117
EPILOGUE   122

PART TWO: Your Journey — 125

PREP STAGE: Your Game Plan — 127
What Investor Type Are You? — 128
Before You Invest: — 130
The Bulls And The Bears Can Both Be Your Friends
STAGE ONE: Get Ready: Mindset, Money, and Mapping — 137
STAGE TWO: Shopping for Assets — 144
How do you pick a good crypto exchange?
STAGE THREE: Perils of the journey – fortify security — 150
STAGE FOUR: Get your Soft Wallet — 167
STAGE FIVE: Time to Trade — 171
STAGE SIX: Don't get misdirected – How to watch your steps — 175
STAGE SEVEN: Safe at Home — 178
To cash out or not cash out Crypto – that is the question 99
STRATEGIES TO CONSIDER — 184
Conclusion — 188
EPILOGUE: Can Crypto Be Tamed? — 191

RESOURCES — 191
Glossary — 192
Medley of Security Resources — 222

Acknowledgments — 225

INTRODUCTION

The Raw Truth: I Felt Really Lost

Dear Reader,

I fully admit it. Like many of you readers, I am a tried-and-true digital immigrant in every sense of the word. What that means is that some of us are fifty-plus, and not that long ago, the IBM electric typewriter was cutting-edge technology. But then the dot-matrix printers arrived that connected to computers (what are those?) that had WordStar installed for word processing, later replaced by Microsoft Word. DOS threw you for a loop, but you probably took at least one, likely confusing, computer programming class just to say you tried. You could mostly hold your own with the three innovations mentioned above until your cassettes and videotapes were made obsolete by CDs and DVDs, which were then quickly replaced with mp3s and Blu-ray, then streaming. You retired your answering machine when VOIP arrived, and your flip phones and BlackBerriesR were quickly commandeered by smartphones.

I sheepishly admit that I still have an answering machine connected to my house's landline for emergencies. Mostly, it collects dust and frustrates the auto-bots that call my home advising me of my outstanding $100,000 IRS tax bill that must be paid to Igor in Russia forthwith with Target gift cards or the police will be arriving at my door to handle the matter directly.

Seriously though, having been in business since college, as a veteran entrepreneur, I begrudgingly shifted from weekly fax machine blasts to email marketing as our new communications system to reach out to customers. At the time, I manufactured a line of single-use disposable garments for the apparel and spa industries under the brand name called TOSS.

Now, creating and leaving a legacy to be proud of is my passion. For that, I wear two hats: one as an investor and the other as a generational wealth strategist and legacy architect. As an investor, I strategically grow investments. As a generational wealth strategist, I speak with people about architecting their own expression of legacy while advocating for a more harmonious approach around optimizing the impact of their family's financial legacy now and in the future. We talk about how a family can craft and execute on a vision of legacy that includes the priorities of the different generations since each generation sees the world through different eyes. Statistics show that many families lose their wealth within as little as three generations. According to the Williams Group wealth consultancy, 70 percent of wealthy families lose their wealth by the second generation. My interest is to disrupt that statistic.

Crypto began to pique my interest a few years ago after hearing about it from friends and the news. I eventually realized that this was a new frontier that I wanted to learn about and possibly venture into. When there's something I don't know much about, as a rule, I reach out to my trusted financial advisors for direction. The reactions I received from them regarding cryptocurrencies and blockchain were not what I had expected. They warned, "Don't do it!" Others advised caution, stating, "I'd stay away from that. There's no basis for its value. Besides, that's for people who launder money." Some even shared personal stories of loss, saying, "I tried it and lost money. It's not good timing."

These were not the answers I anticipated, but I respected their concern. Too many people were betting too heavily on crypto and losing. My advisors are experts at allocating money into value investments that preserve capital, not take unnecessary risk for high returns. I saw crypto as a different animal. For me, it represented a new economic system that needed to be studied to enter into it correctly. Since they saw risk and volatility, not value, when it came to crypto, I knew that my only way into this rising asset class was learning it myself. Because of its volatility, I knew that I needed to approach it with extreme caution.

Why does understanding crypto matter? Simple. The returns have outrun the growth of traditional stock markets by crazy percentages and I believe that blockchain, the technology behind crypto, will revolutionize our economic futures.

Case in point, the Standard & Poor's 500 (S&P 500) index's average annualized return is around 10%. Bitcoin, since its inception in 2009, has risen 9,000,000%.[1] This return is not a typo! After triple-checking the numbers and confirming them with various financial sources including Bloomberg, these never-seen-before returns have made more overnight billionaires and millionaires in the entire history of investing. This growth is jaw-dropping! Yet, it's been hard to determine. Are these fly by night returns too good to be true, or are they a dizzyingly rewarding anomaly for early investors? My financial advisors landed on the side of skepticism.

I, on the other hand, took a step beyond conventional investing and dug in. From where I was standing, digital assets and the cryptocurrency economy, with its decentralized financial systems and protocols (DeFi),

---

[1] V. Hajric, "Bitcoin's 9,000,000% Rise This Decade Leaves the Skeptics Aghast," Bloomberg, December 31, 2019, https://www.bloomberg.com/news/articles/2019-12-31/bitcoin-s-9-000-000-rise-this-decade-leaves-the-skeptics-aghast#xj4y7vzkg. Accessed: June 18, 2023.

made financial transactions more efficient, faster, and safer than the systems the traditional banks currently offer. If history was any indication (think of ATMs), this disruptive technology could, at some point, see mass adoption too. I also recognize that cryptocurrencies, as decentralized digital assets, could be here for a short time and then eventually evolve into something entirely different. Whatever the future holds, I saw a window of opportunity that is open now.

Candidly, this frontier was foreign to me. I had no idea how to navigate crypto and blockchain technology or reconcile their quantum pace of change. So, I did what I always do with new frontiers. I researched, registered for a class, found some pros, and invested a small amount of "mad money," so I could develop enough savvy to stand on my own two feet as a new digital asset investor.

> **SIDE NOTE**
>
> *What is mad money? It's your Vegas money, that amount you don't mind risking when you play blackjack or the slots for a night or two. Since I'm not a Vegas girl, I used my annual latte fund. That was an amount that I wouldn't miss if I lost it. So, enjoy the journey, and begin with your mad money should you decide to give digital assets a test drive.*

In my own process, I took in a lot of information fast, gained valuable insights, and, even with some missteps, started to earn small profits. Understanding the global reach that blockchain and crypto have, I believe that digital currencies of all kinds will become an integral part of how we purchase and invest. As a trustee, I saw the importance of allocating a small portion of the trusts' resources into the blockchain domain. To justify investing in such a speculative sector, I needed solid reasons supporting the merits of investing in crypto now versus later, especially with its level of volatility. Unlike traditionally steady investments like index funds, investing in blockchain and digital assets calls for a different approach.

Why Taming Crypto?

Taming Crypto is a digestible, straightforward primer that guides and supports digital immigrants who, like myself, are curious about blockchain and crypto and want help to simply know where to begin. It's the book I desperately needed but could not find when I first started learning about digital assets. I searched far and wide, from LAX to London, Oslo to Dubai, even venturing as far as the Seychelles Islands. What I did find were books filled with crypto jargon written by techie brainiacs for fellow techie brainiacs. I might as well have been reading Greek! The books were literal fire hoses of information that were hard to fully process. I was no closer to understanding this new digital frontier with its unique rules, language, and mindset.

    To ground myself in the basics, I read what I could, studied with experts, and bought some crypto. Friends quickly became interested in my crypto journey when I explained why they should care and how it related to their lives. I shared details about blockchain and cryptocurrencies with metaphors about the Wild West. That worked! People who knew nothing about the topic and were truly crypto newbies, were understanding me and even sharing the basics with others using those same metaphors. Music to my ears!

In my wanderings, I was running into more and more people who were open to crypto and wanted to develop enough confidence to purchase a small amount for themselves. This exciting trend inspired me to write this book. I was eager to create a beginner's roadmap that breaks concepts down into a step-by-step process that's motivating and easy enough to implement.

At first glance, cryptocurrency may seem like just another transactional system for buying and selling that happens to bypass traditional banking systems. But the underlying technology of blockchain offers so much more. When coupled with Artificial Intelligence (AI), the synergy of blockchain and AI promises to reshape every aspect of our world. Becoming educated about crypto and the foundational blockchain technology not only makes it possible to invest intelligently in future technologies, but also prepares us for the uncharted territories that lie ahead.

My hope is that *Taming Crypto* will equip you with the fundamental knowledge and basic tools to explore crypto as a potential digital asset investment incrementally and safely. At its core, this book is a primer that sheds light on ways to leverage the rapid advancements blockchain is bringing. Whether you are a crypto-curious beginner or a digital asset veteran wanting to deepen your understanding, this book will help you navigate the new digital frontier.

MEET The FOMOs

Like most any author, I have a vivid imagination. As a trustee involved in finance and education, there's nothing more rewarding than inspiring those who love to learn. So, one evening, while reading yet another eye-crossing crypto book, it dawned on me that I could do better. I could write a book that most anyone could actually understand and would not want to put down. And I could help anyone wanting to understand the fundamentals of buying, holding, and trading cryptocurrency while learning how to up-level their digital security practices.

I slowly marinated on ways that would quickly engage readers while providing a starting roadmap. Many media outlets refer to cryptocurrencies and their exchanges as another new frontier, regularly dubbing the industry as the new "Wild West". And like the Wild West, this frontier is untamed, unpredictable and brimming with drama, visionaries, tycoons, innovators, bandits, and pioneers who courageously take the daring step to be the first ones in to stake their claim, risking it all for the possibility of great fortunes.

In developing the story, I was brainstorming with my collaborator about popular names from frontier times. In the flash of a moment, inspiration struck. The FOMO Family! That would be the name of the main characters, a tongue-in-cheek allusion to the pervasive "Fear of Missing Out" (FOMO) that runs rampant today like an epidemic, especially in the cryptocurrency world.

I then closed my eyes, sensing the frenetic energy of the cryptocurrency movement, visualizing hordes of people madly rushing to be the first ones in, and how almost everyone I'd met in the space had yet another coin that would be the next biggest hit or the next colossal disaster. Daily,

I felt an undercurrent of anxiety, wondering if I was too late in the game. Was I behind? Had I already missed out? There was no denying it. I had FOMO! Maybe some of you can relate!

This primer uses a tall tale to paint a picture for you rather than robotically explaining digital asset fundamentals, and explores different aspects of this new economy. Your thinking and your comfort level might be challenged. In the story, the FOMOs muster the courage and willpower to embark into the untamed frontier. As modern-day pioneers, we are constantly honed by the challenges that mark the unfamiliar frontiers of our lives.

On their new frontier, the FOMOs face similar challenges as the pioneers and ranchers of yesteryear. This new frontier has its own protocols, attitudes, and mindsets that demand a high level of resilience and adaptability. In their determination to leave a dismal situation, the FOMOs exhibit the same resilience that the Wild West demanded. Just as with anything new we are pioneering, in the digital world, resilience means looking with new eyes, releasing what we think we know, accepting change, and letting go of our expectations about how things ought to be. And let me reassure you now, dear reader, that if you feel FOMO too, crypto and blockchain are still young. You're not too late. In fact, you're right on time.

Getting the Lay of the Land

Because this book serves crypto beginners and veterans alike, it's not essential to read it cover-to-cover. For the new and crypto-curious, I share the fundamentals to ground you right away. You, specifically, would be served to read the whole book.

For everyone else who has some level of involvement with crypto and blockchain, the first part of this book is more of a quick review. For those of you interested in a step-by-step approach to exploring the intricacies of crypto, this book has that. Even seasoned investors can find value (and delight) in this comprehensive primer, as it offers insightful content using humorous anecdotes as the fictional training ground for learning more about trading digital assets.

My Dilemma

The dilemma I faced in writing *Taming Crypto* was finding the right balance between simplifying the content without compromising accuracy. I dedicated many months engaging in conversations with both experts and newcomers to the subject. By decoding the complexities together, we arrived at a seven stage structure for the FOMO Family's journey as well as for yours in the pursuit to becoming a savvy digital investor.

This book is my humble attempt at addressing that dilemma. I ask some modicum of forgiveness if it falls short. At the very least, I hope to entertain you on your exploration as you learn about crypto investing and blockchain in general.

THE SEVEN STAGES TO TAMING CRYPTO

STAGE ONE	Get Ready: Mindset, Money, and Mapping
STAGE TWO	Shopping for Assets
STAGE THREE	Perils of the Journey
STAGE FOUR	Get the Soft Wallet
STAGE FIVE	Time to Trade
STAGE SIX	Don't Get Misdirected!
STAGE SEVEN	Safe at Home

Where should you start reading?

If you are versed in crypto and blockchain, the next chapter is a quick review. Skim it, then go to the heading, "**Are you ready to get wild?**"

If you're a crypto beginner or could use a refresher on crypto and blockchain definitions, then simply carry on from here. In the next chapter, I cover basic concepts to get you started as you enter the new digital frontier..

Crypto Newbies, Start Here

Hello, again!
Welcome to the fascinating world of crypto. In this chapter, we explore, from a bird's eye view, what makes crypto different from traditional money. We'll delve into the concepts of blockchain, the foundation of crypto, and its potential to revolutionize the banking system. Additionally, we'll discuss the trailblazer of cryptocurrency, Bitcoin, as well as have a quick discussion on stablecoins, the difference between Ethereum and

Bitcoin, and the importance of wallets and exchanges. So, let's get started unraveling the wonders of the crypto universe!

What Is Crypto and How Is It Different from Money?

"Crypto," short for cryptocurrency, is a form of money that exists solely in the digital world. It has no tangible representation like an actual dollar bill. By way of example, traditional money, such as the U.S. dollar and the Mexican peso are currencies we can hold in our wallets as bills. They are created and controlled by the government and its banking systems. Cryptocurrencies are outside the banking system—in other words, decentralized—and are created by private companies and citizens, which means central authorities like banks do not govern these transactions. This might only last for a while, however, because governments around the world are beginning to create their own nationalized digital coins. The benefits of using cryptocurrencies are transparency, accessibility, and the fact that transactions can cross borders quickly and inexpensively as compared to sending and receiving bank wires or using Western Union.

Bitcoin: The Trailblazer

Bitcoin, the first-ever cryptocurrency, emerged as a groundbreaking invention that revolutionized the concept of digital money. Created by the mysterious Satoshi Nakamoto, Bitcoin enables secure and private transactions without the need for intermediaries like banks. Its decentralized nature and innovations in blockchain technology gained popularity, especially in the world of tech, setting the stage for the development of numerous other cryptocurrencies.

Blockchain: The Technology Behind Crypto

The foundation of crypto is "blockchain," a revolutionary technology that serves as a digital ledger for recording transactions indefinitely. Think of it as an immutable (unchangeable) accounting ledger where every transaction is recorded permanently, and anyone can verify any transaction recorded on these blockchains. Unlike traditional accounting ledgers controlled by singular entities, blockchain is maintained by a global network of computers. This decentralized infrastructure brings a combination of a security, transparency, and integrity to crypto transactions. Although blockchain technology is the underpinning of cryptocurrencies, it can also be used for a variety of other applications, such as supply chain management, voting systems, digital identity management, and much more.

How Crypto Challenges the Centralized Banking System

One of the most interesting aspects of crypto is its potential to disrupt the centralized banking system and compel its reinvention. Traditionally, financial transactions have been enabled through intermediaries like banks and financial houses that are "centralized." However, with technologies like DeFi (decentralized finance), it's possible to directly borrow, lend, and trade money without banks or other intermediaries. This decentralized approach empowers individuals by saving time with faster transactions and reducing transaction fees. Crypto and DeFi also promote financial inclusion through cellphone apps that offer services to those without access to traditional banking systems.

The Importance of Wallets and Exchanges

To engage with crypto, we need to talk about crypto exchanges and digital asset wallets. Wallets digitally store crypto assets. "Hardware wallets" secure the keys (codes) to the assets offline, whereas "software wallets" secure the keys (codes) to assets online. Soft wallets are very convenient to access and use. Still, they are considered more vulnerable to hackers than hard wallets because they are always connected to the internet on our phones or computers. Crypto exchanges are platforms for buying, selling, and trading cryptocurrencies.

Cryptocurrency Coins Versus Tokens: What's the difference?

To confuse you just a bit more (LOL), there are coins and tokens. Both are digital currencies that can be bought, sold, and traded. The difference is that a crypto coin is a digital currency that operates on its own blockchain. Bitcoin (BTC) and Ethereum (ETH) are examples of that because BTC and ETH are "native" cryptocurrencies to their own blockchains. That means Bitcoin is the native coin that is on the Bitcoin blockchain, while Ethereum is the native coin on the Ethereum blockchain.

Tokens, on the other hand, are digital currencies built off the technology of a blockchain that is already established. There are many tokens associated with (or that comply with) the Ethereum blockchain. These tokens are known as ERC-20 tokens. A few examples of ERC-20 tokens are Tether, USD Coin, Shiba Inu, and DAI.

Our cell phones with their countless number of apps can help us understand. Our mobile phones have apps that are specifically engineered for their specific operating system. For example, an Apple phone uses its iOS operating system. The iOS system has apps that are native to Apple, like Safari and Apple Music. These apps were created by Apple for their iOS operating system.

A "token" is like a third-party app (like Spotify or YouTube). These aren't created by the operating system's designers, but they are developed to work on it. Just as third-party apps rely on the existing operating system to function, tokens rely on an existing blockchain for their operation and functionality.

Exploring Stablecoins, Ethereum, and Bitcoin[2]

Each cryptocurrency or crypto token is built on a specific blockchain. Each one of these blockchains provides a digital infrastructure that empowers, activates, or supports specific cryptocurrencies. Let's look closely at stablecoins, Ethereum, and Bitcoin and their underlying blockchains.

- **Stablecoins** were developed as a stable currency that does not change in value when the market moves. They are often pegged to a real-world asset like the U.S. dollar. Stablecoins can work with, as in be built on, any number of the blockchains like Ethereum, Binance Smart Chain, or Solana. Since each blockchain contains specific technology that meets different goals, which blockchain is chosen as the foundational technology depends on a few considerations, like how big it needs to scale (scalability), security, and the specific features that the stablecoin is meant to provide for its functionality or utility.

---

[2] Definitions generated or vetted by ChatGPT, 2023, OpenAI, https://chat.openai.com. Rewritten for style and content.

- **Ethereum** is a top 10 cryptocurrency that is the native cryptocurrency to its own blockchain. Ethereum, as a blockchain, is a decentralized platform that supports many decentralized applications (DApps). It also is used by developers as the foundation to create many different crypto tokens.

- **Bitcoin**, the true pioneer of cryptocurrency, also has its own blockchain. The Bitcoin blockchain was the first iteration of blockchain technology, giving the world a decentralized system for recording Bitcoin transactions on a digital ledger. The Bitcoin blockchain was developed to facilitate peer-to-peer (you to me with no bank in the middle) electronic cash transactions as well as to serve as a secure ledger that records with full transparency any transaction, making it seamless to both track the ownership of and transfer of Bitcoin.

How Is Bitcoin Mined with Algorithms?

Bitcoin mining, like gold mining, involves the extraction of a valuable resource. However, instead of physical labor, it requires computing power to solve complex mathematical problems, known as algorithms. When these algorithms are solved, new Bitcoin are created.

Just as gold mining is a challenging process that requires the right conditions, tools, and equipment, so too is Bitcoin mining. However, in the case of Bitcoin, the "mining" is performed digitally by computers. These computers are supercomputers that complete the hardest of computations (just like miners use all their might to dig with a pickaxe inside a gold mine) to solve the mathematical problems that ultimately yield Bitcoin—the digital equivalent of gold.

The "refining" process in gold mining can also be likened to the process of validating Bitcoin transactions and ensuring that the new Bitcoin adheres to the rules of the system. This validation protocol legitimizes each Bitcoin, ensuring that the newly minted Bitcoin can be traded or sold on a cryptocurrency exchange, just as gold is refined so it can be sold on the open market.

In summary, while the processes of gold mining and Bitcoin mining are different in absolute terms, the concept of extracting and refining a valuable commodity to make it market-ready is what they share in common. Bitcoin mining is the digital parallel to gold mining, with computers replacing physical labor, solving complex mathematical problems to create or "mint" a new Bitcoin.

Keep Riding the Trail! Don't Stop Now.

Congratulations on getting started! I know this section gives you a few new distinctions to ponder. *Don't worry.* It might take a bit for the definitions to sink in. As you continue on and read the tale of the FOMOs, they will. Very soon, you'll understand these basics as you keep on the journey.

Are You Ready to Get Wild?

Now, close your eyes and imagine… no, wait, keep your eyes open; you'll need them to read. The Wild West attracted renegades looking to mine for riches after hearing word of fortunes made from the gold rush in the west. Now, imagine that the world of cryptocurrency is a new frontier with no sheriff, one main trail, and lots of characters, where one never knows what will happen next.

Doesn't that sound like crypto to you? It does to me!

I invite you to see this new world in your mind's eye.

In real life, to acquire cryptocurrency, you log onto an exchange. In this new, imagined world, the equivalent of the crypto exchange is what I call the "auction house." Whereas on a crypto exchange, you trade cryptocurrencies, in the auction house, you trade horses. To safely store your crypto, you use a digital wallet. To safely store your horses, you keep them on a ranch.

As you'll read in the FOMOs' story, venturing into this new frontier took moxie and courage! Anyone who dares must saddle up and adopt that good ol' fashioned "Wild West" mentality. Ready to meet the FOMOs? Then, let's head 'em on out!

Fondly,

Maryl Gladstone

P.S. Stay on the trail. This is just getting good!

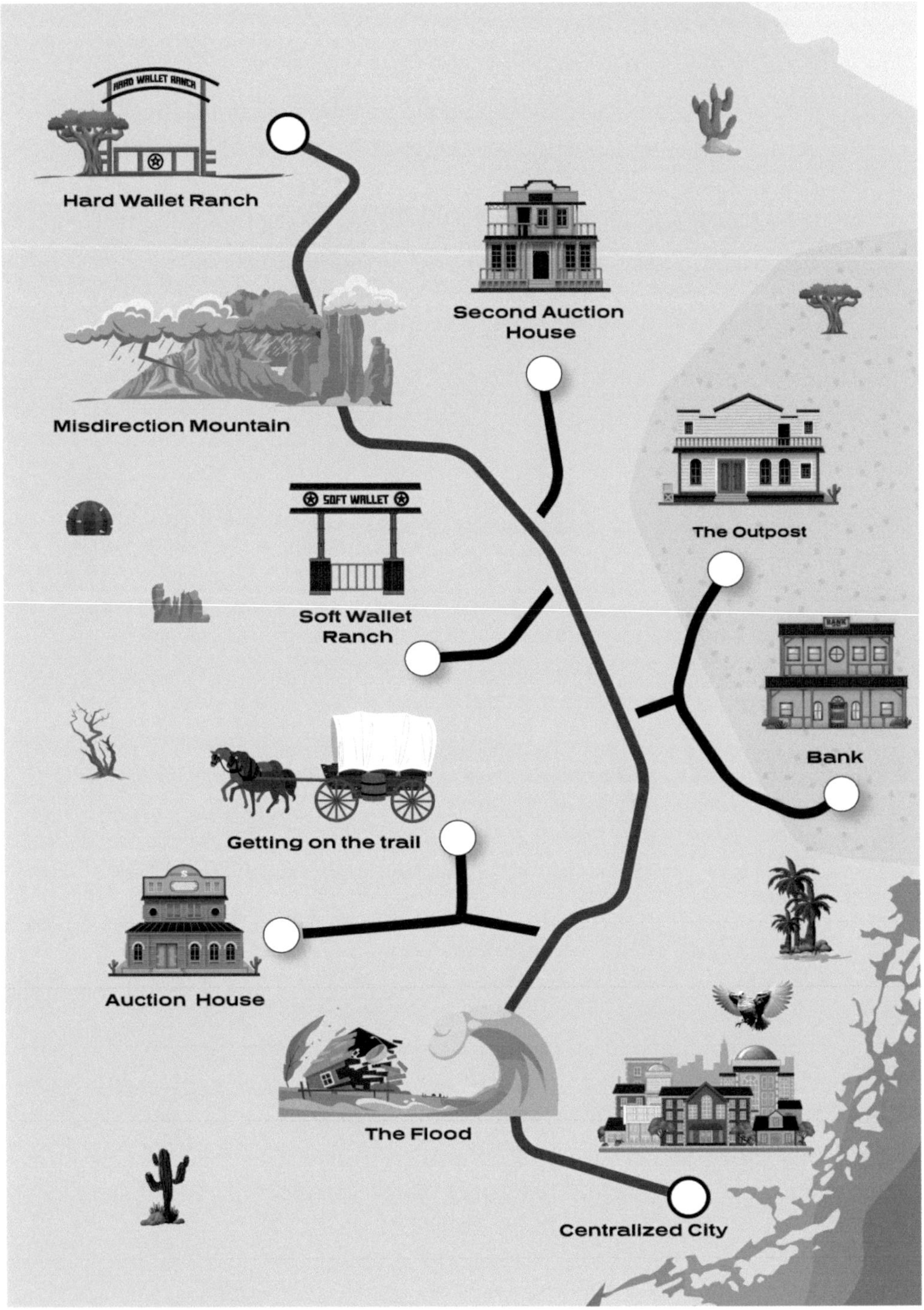

PART ONE
The Story of the FOMOs

> *In the wild, there is no safety net. You must tread lightly—but live boldly.*
>
> —EDWARD MICHAEL "BEAR" GRYLLS, ADVENTURER & WRITER

Introducing Centralized City

Centralized City, the capital of the region, was run like a well-oiled machine. It extended across the eastern section of the land and was bordered by the sea. Its governing council conducted the city's business. Because Centralized City had become a well-known haven for pilgrims migrating from far and wide, the council faced challenges beyond what they could imagine or were prepared for. To address the increasing influx of newcomers, the governing council instituted a mandate that every one of them would be fed, housed, and equipped with their very own "Pigeon Phone" (like the cellphones of today).

Presenting the Pigeon Phone 1.0

Who knew that a carrier pigeon could double as a communication device? The Pigeon Phone 1.0 is a distant cousin to the carrier pigeon with technological modifications.

The number of city folk increased exponentially! This new influx of people made governance more complex, causing the need for more ordinances to provide safety and security. There were now so many regulations

that even laughing after 5 p.m. could result in a citation. The governing council was even forced to legislate the lighting of candles at sundown. Noise levels and air quality had become serious problems!

The council was founded to promote the general welfare, a tall order to be sure. While the older folks didn't mind complying with the amassing ordinances, the younger generations were unhappy with the continuous piling on of rules. Rather than seeing their benefits, they felt constrained by them and protested weekly in the town square.

Meet the FOMOs

As long-standing residents of Centralized City, the FOMOs were a motley bunch of good-hearted humans. For many generations, the FOMO Family had deep roots in Centralized City that kept them bound there. They also shared a natural ability to manage, create, and maintain financial ledgers, skills that were passed down through the generations. Today, they'd be known as accountants.

Joseph FOMO, cautious by nature, always had his family's best interests at heart. A wiz with numbers, he spoke the budgeting language better than anyone else in the family. Ma and Pa FOMO had instilled in him the core values of honor, honesty, integrity, and obedience. He was a man who rarely took chances and was quite conservative with decisions when faced with danger or risk.

Joseph's cousin **Freddie FOMO** (short for Frederica) was the most respected and revered pioneer woman of her day. Both famous and infamous, most folks would rather face a bear than deal with Freddie on one of her bad days! She lived far away from the Centralized City limits and, over the years, had become a highly accomplished rancher and horse breeder. She owned several ranches in both the Soft Wallet Ranch and Hard Wallet Ranch Territories.

Maverick, Freddie's closest confidante, was not a FOMO, but he was beloved by Freddie, so he gets an honorable mention here. He took her under his wings, ensuring her ranches were right next to his in both the Soft and Hard Wallet Ranch Territories. Across the land, he was known as a fearless frontier guide and one heck of a talented engineer. Rumor has it he was one of the inventors of the Pigeon Phones.

Let's Get to Know a Few More FOMOs...

Emma FOMO, Joseph's wife, was clever and never shied away from a card game. Having grown up in the countryside, she could farm in her sleep. When she visited her grandmother in the city on weekends, Emma worked at the local emporium, which is where Joseph first set eyes on her. Very quickly, the two teenagers turned into smitten lovebirds, marrying at the ripe young age of eighteen. After their nuptials, Joseph and Emma moved to her family's farm, caring for the animals and tending to the crops their family had been growing for generations.

Although Joseph FOMO was more conventional and cautious than Emma, he still had a spirited zest for life. Regarding physical labor, he could handle a rifle when absolutely necessary, but mostly he was numerically inclined, like his father and grandfather before him. From a very early age, it was clear that ledger management would also be Joseph's profession. A highly linear thinker, Joseph flourished with predictability, preferring consistency over surprises. Like any true maximizer, he was naturally compelled to consider every fact about any matter before plunging into it. The unknowns were, frankly, troublesome. Reluctantly at first, Joseph stepped into the farm life with Emma, eventually taking over managing the books, with Emma overseeing the farming operations.

Soon **FOMO Junior** arrived.

After a few years of tending the farm, Joseph and Emma had a little bun in the oven, and FOMO Junior was born. As he grew, Junior developed a love for animals and a penchant for discovering new "lands." A natural adventurer, he drew maps in the sand of where he had just been, daydreaming about his next adventure during his lessons.

Caring for a little one while running the farm proved more than Joseph and Emma could handle, so when FOMO Junior turned five, they returned to Centralized City, moving in with Joseph's parents. Ma and Pa FOMO had a modest brownstone, making for very cramped living quarters. Joseph struggled with moving back in with Ma and Pa because change unnerved him. They eventually settled into life in the city but missed country life and longed for a place to call their own.

Ma and Pa were very much set in their ways, thriving from the status quo. They liked the safety of routines and had grown accustomed to the rhythm of Centralized City. They believed that following rules would ensure a good life, and they counted on matters of the city being managed by the governing council. Loyal to the core, they stood behind all the council's decisions for the region, appreciating the systems and structures that benefited the collective. If they had to make a choice, they'd accept less for themselves over changing directions, even if that meant moving into ever-smaller quarters to make room for the onslaught of newcomers, because having enough to get by, feeling a sense of security, and showing loyalty were the three things that mattered most.

A Visit with Freddie FOMO

Freddie FOMO was Joseph's favorite cousin. Growing up as wee bits, they were inseparable, and as adults, their bond held firm. Sometimes, under the light of the moon, Freddie would reminisce about the secret watering hole she and Joseph swam in after supper with their friends as young'uns and how they would finish off one of Ma FOMO's red cream pies all by themselves, then blame it on the dog so as not get a whooping!

Now a woman, Freddie had lost her husband in an accident, and after a dark period of mourning, she took their young son, Shane, and set up ranching operations in both the Soft Wallet Ranch and Hard Wallet Ranch Territories. To expand her horse breeding business, twice a year in the spring and the fall, Freddie took horse-buying trips, traveling to the two biggest auction houses across the land. This time around, she was in the market for some very specialized horse breeds that she could only find at the auction house in Centralized City.

It had been many years since Freddie and Joseph had seen each other. Freddie had heard that her cousin had moved back from Emma's family farm to Centralized City and was eager to see him again. Upon entering the city, she called Joseph. Hearing Freddie's voice, Joseph could barely contain himself! He had missed her so much, and they all had much to catch up on!

"Joseph!" Freddie said with relief. "Freddie! Is it really you?!" Freddie continued. "It's me! I just got to the city. Let's meet! It's been so long!" "Yes," Joseph agreed. "What are y'all doing now? Emma and I think about you and Shane all the time." Freddie heard his worry. "Joseph, Shane, and I are doing well."

Freddie continued, "After my beloved Phillip died in that terrible accident, we had many somber days. We felt adrift without him, but something inside was nagging me to seek out a new path outside of city life for us. Where that road lay was foggy for a time, but there was one thing I knew I was made for: breeding horses and running a ranch like I did with my family before I had ever met Phillip. And Shane has taken to ranching like a natural."

Being both a young widow and a new mother had been a tough go. With Shane in tow, Freddie found a guide named Maverick, who led them into the frontier. Being that she was a lady, he was initially reluctant to guide them. But Maverick quickly saw that she was smart and feisty as hellfire, so he agreed to help them get their ranches.

Freddie didn't want another day to pass without seeing her cousin. "Joseph, let's get together tomorrow, and I'll tell your more."

They agreed to meet. Hearing Freddie's story deeply agitated Joseph. On the one hand, he couldn't imagine how Freddie could put herself and Shane in harm's way! Everyone knows that the frontier is dangerous! On the other hand, his love for Freddie gave him pause. Yes, he was vexed, but he was equally inspired by her recounting. In truth, a part of him envied her freedom and adventurous spirit. Her triumph was causing him to think differently. Change usually made his head spin, but if Freddie could leave the city life, maybe they could too, someday.

Meeting the Following Afternoon

The following afternoon, Joseph and Emma met Freddie under the bell tower in the square. Freddie couldn't wait to share about her day. Bubbling with passion, she excitedly explained, "We just picked up some new horses at auction! To expand, we've added cattle and farming to our operations. We also recently found gold nuggets in our creek! The Hard Wallet Ranch Territory is the best, bar none! The land is so protected that those crypto-jacking horse thieves still haven't put their scheming hands on our most valuable horses! But we couldn't be making so much progress without our other ranch in the Soft Wallet Ranch Territory. That's the ranch where we keep certain horses and Tether ponies for trading. Would you like to go to the auction house now, so I can show you the new horses I bid on?"

"Freddie, yes, we would love to see the horses, but can we do it in the morning?" Emma asked noticing the subtle sweat on Joseph's brow. Meeting his gaze, she turned back to Freddie, standing her ground with her to assuage his nervousness. "We do want to hear about what you're doing next. We talk about breeding horses now and again, but Joseph thinks it is too soon to focus on any of that. Freddie, I have to say that with the many dangers of the trail, what you've done is incredible."

"Emma, do you realize how many city folks are becoming pioneers and new ranchers on the frontier?" Freddie continued, "As for running a ranch, I've built a good system for that now. I'll teach y'all my approach if you have an interest. You'll learn about auction houses and horse breeding, as well as trading on the frontier. We've had our tough times, but now our breeding program is ace-high amazing and expanding! Our horse herds are growing and getting more valuable with time because we know how to buy right."

Joseph grappled with all that Freddie was sharing. "Weren't you nervous about getting attacked on the trail?"

"Joseph," Freddie responded, "the trail was rough, but we stayed out of harm's way. Maverick kept us safe and left nothing to chance. He helped us find our first ranch by his in the Soft Wallet Ranch Territory. We got ourselves settled and rested while he tended to his own herd on his Soft Wallet ranch. After a bit, we continued with him into the Hard Wallet Ranch Territory, where we acquired another ranch. So yes, it's hard and risky. But now we have successful ranches in both territories. My biggest and best ranch is further west in the Hard Wallet Ranch Territory."

Freddie paused, closing her eyes, remembering that moment when she first set eyes on the land. "The ranch is surrounded by mountains, has a gentle river for the horses to drink from, and has farmland shining gold in flax. We now have horses, colts, and cattle, and the land extends far beyond what the eye can see. That's how things are now, but it all took time." Emma let that image blanket over her as she imagined what that would be like for her family too.

Freddie carried on. "In the beginning, I didn't know if what I was doing was right. But it turned out right for us. For that I'm grateful. Just know that I'll walk you through each step we took so you understand what it actually takes to set up ranches on the frontier. There's no need to rush anything. I really love you and want you to know about the grand opportunities the frontier has for new ranchers and why so many are taking to the Blockchain Trail.

City folk who travel on their own with no guide are fools. That wouldn't be you. Y'all would have Maverick to guide you. He'll get you to my ranch safely if you visit. He's a well-known frontier guide who knows his way, he knows his horses, and he's the best there is."

They all agreed to meet again the following day.

Joseph and Emma were intrigued but also overwhelmed by Freddie's story. It was a lot to take in, but it had them rethinking everything. What they "knew" about the new frontier came from rumors or warnings of danger from the governing council. Freddie's words didn't paint pictures of sweet lullabies and Sunday picnics, but it wasn't so frightening to hear her tell it. Joseph and Emma walked in silence as they held each other tight, heading back home.

That night, they both dreamt of a hat-wearing, boot-scooting, tall, shadowy figure guiding them through the frontier. Their dreamstate was abruptly interrupted by their worst nightmare.

The Flood That Changed It All

The nightmare was real! That evening, at midnight, Centralized City was suddenly besieged by a turn of weather that thrust the entire region into complete mayhem! The skies were thick and foreboding, turning incessant rain into a deluge that became a monsoon with hail the size of oranges, denting rooftops and Mother Earth alike. This would come to be known as the worst storm Centralized City had ever seen! Sadly, despite a multitude of city ordinances, flood management had not yet been addressed.

The sound of hail smashing into their roof abruptly woke Emma and Joseph. Jolting straight up, they moved to the bedroom window, immediately realizing that they were ankle-deep in freezing water. They panicked! The house was flooding! There was the unmistakable sound of breaking glass and screaming from their neighbors' homes. They watched frenzied animals float by their window, clinging to whatever they could get their paws on. Having mere moments to find Junior, Emma and Joseph made it to his room, and Joseph snatched him out of bed, with all three of them struggling to get to higher ground. Emma had the presence of mind to grab their Pigeon Phone. The only safe spot within immediate reach was their son's tree house in the oak tree outside their bedroom window. Terrified, they quickly climbed out into the tree. Joseph would not let go of Junior. The thought of his son drowning had him tighten his grip around the boy even harder. When they regained just the slightest bit of composure, they watched the havoc from up high, seeing the water carry away things they once held dear. Panic again ensued when they realized that they had no idea if Ma and Pa were alive and could even be stuck in the cold and murky waters. The call Emma made to Ma and Pa's Pigeon Phone kept ringing. No answer. Soaked and feeling utterly helpless, it was almost more than they could take as they looked into the eye of the storm. They continued to be pummeled by the rain pouring down from the dark, gloomy sky. Each hour the storm raged on was one more nail in the coffin of the FOMOs' life as they had known it.

Meanwhile, Freddie to the Rescue

Freddie's favorite boarding house was situated on the outskirts of town, directly across from the bank and the city's main auction house. The storm was violent, but the boarding house was on high ground, so she had no idea that the FOMOs' house was almost entirely submerged under water. She called Joseph when she realized the extreme danger they might be in. Thank the high heavens that Joseph and his family were soaking wet but safe!

As the rain slowed, Freddie got help to retrieve Joseph and his family. As the rescue crew made its way into the city, she promised the distressed Joseph that she would find out about his Ma and Pa. She called their Pigeon Phone, just as Joseph had, and when there was an answer, she breathed a huge sigh of relief. "Auntie, thank heavens you answered! Joseph has been trying to reach you and he won't rest until he knows that you're both safe! Where are you? I'm coming now with help to bring y'all to higher ground."

"I'm sorry," said the voice on the other end of the line. "This is not Joseph's ma. I'm their neighbor. I'm afraid I have terrible news . . ."

Freddie dropped her head into her hand as the neighbor explained what had happened. Ma and Pa thought they'd be safe if they climbed to the roof, but they slipped as they climbed and were swept away by the flood, and the pigeon flew right onto the neighbor's right shoulder. They floated to a nearby tree and managed to hold onto each other for a few hours but were carried away as the water level rose.

The neighbor had been on her own roof, calling to get help for the elderly couple, and saw the whole thing. "They hung on to each other 'till the very end," she said. Freddie thanked her quietly and ended the call.

When Freddie arrived, she found Joseph and Emma in shock, so she put off telling Joseph about his folks' demise. Freddie and the crew had one goal: to save the survivors. They got Joseph and his family from the platform onto a small boat. By the time they reached the boarding house, Joseph had become frantic to know the whereabouts of my folks. "Did you find out anything, Freddie? Anything?" he pleaded.

"Let's get you into some dry clothes, and I'll see what else I can find out," Freddie said, wanting to distract them just a bit longer.

"Freddie!" Emma shouted. "Where are Ma and Pa?"

Freddie stopped short, and with tears and anguish, turned around. "Cousins," she began, "I'm just as sorry as I can be . . ."

Freddie relayed the story she had heard from Ma and Pa's neighbor. Joseph and Emma's worst fears had been realized. Everyone stood in stunned silence, still dripping wet from the storm. Broken by fear and exhaustion, FOMO Junior fell to the ground and fainted. Realizing that he would never see his grandparents again was more than his little heart could bear.

What Were the FOMOs to Do?

The FOMOs situated themselves in a small room next to Freddie's in the boardinghouse. They changed into dry clothes and drank some hot coffee to chase away the chill. Freddie then talked to Joseph and Emma away from Junior.

"Joseph, Emma, I'm guessing that you'd rather not discuss this now, and I mean no disrespect to your Ma and Pa, but we need to talk. The flood has put Centralized City in shambles. The locals are saying that Main Street is still a river. The raging water sent uprooted trees and all sorts of drowned animals floating down the street, leaving a trail of total destruction. Even if the city is rebuilt, it will take months just to clear away the mud. I'm afraid what's left of the city is chaos."

Freddie hated to push after such tragedy, but she knew this was a pivotal moment. If ever there was a time to take to the frontier, it was now.

"Freddie, I can't think right now!" Joseph exclaimed. "My head is swirling. My ma and pa are gone. The house is in ruins. With the entire city flooded, my work here is done." Freddie felt his heartbreak and vowed to do whatever she could to help them through this. "Joseph, I can help you start anew. I promise. I'm here for you now."

Although the timing was terrible, it was their watershed moment. In too much shock to see it, the fate of the FOMOs was now at a crossroad. Freddie knew that her cousin needed her strength and direction more than ever. She wanted them near her, but to get them oriented with the frontier, she would need to address the harsh realities of the trail. "Joseph, Emma, this is fate's finger pointing you west. I know it's hard to see past the damage of the storm, but you've been saving and saving so you could get a farm and ranch of your own. I'll help you. You'll make your Ma and Pa proud."

Joseph knew that Emma would get behind any decision for their small family. Freddie went silent for what seemed like an eternity, realizing what she said next would not make this decision any easier. "Y'all are going to need to prepare yourselves; the frontier is a tough and lawless place. In the city, there are rules. Once you leave the city, anything can happen. You need to do whatever it takes to protect yourselves, to stay out of harm's way, and to fend off predators and bandits."

Freddie knew they could do it. There was a smart way to make it on the frontier, and there was a way to lose it all. Freddie's way meant having a plan for finding the best ranches, a great guide, a detailed map, the right equipment, supplies, and horses, and lots of coins hidden underneath the wagon. They would need to take it in steps and stages.

Emotionally spent, Joseph knew he had to take all this in.

"By the time you finish the last step, you'll have a main house with a porch on both of your ranches, with your herds of horses, right by me. I already know how we can set you up."

Freddie wasn't just talking. She had traveled this journey, and for her and Shane, it had been the right choice for their future all those years ago. Staying in the city would have constrained them. Had they stayed, she and Shane would never have known the vast beauty of the frontier or the freedom of taking that unforged path. Like everyone in the city, they would have lived at the behest of the governing council. Shane would never have hunted, built fences for the horses, or been a part of creating new communities with other ranchers. He was now strong and tough and could weather any storm, and he was still a young man!

Even though they would be deeply grieving and ranching would challenge them to their core, Freddie knew that Emma and Joseph had the instincts, the drive, and the intelligence to make it in the new frontier. And, if and when they made it, they would experience freedom and prosperity the likes of which they'd never known before. That is what made being a rancher in the Hard Wallet Ranch Territory so profoundly rewarding. For Freddie, the new frontier was the Promised Land for future generations.

As shell-shocked as they were, Joseph and Emma knew that pivoting and going west would change their destiny. Ma and Pa had never once considered leaving Centralized City, and maybe that was their fate, but this was a moment of truth for the FOMOs. Joseph needed to step away to process all of this. His stomach was in knots. Leaving the city and taking to the trail was well beyond his comfort zone. The frontier could be dangerous! He'd be putting his family in harm's way and at great financial risk because this new life would require a good portion of their savings. They could fail and lose all they would invest to leave.

Joseph stepped outside. It was now daylight, but there was no sun in the sky, only impossible darkness over the expanse of the city. Joseph paused to breathe and started walking almost aimlessly. He needed to think. A man like Joseph doesn't put his entire life savings at risk for anything.

If they stayed in Centralized City, in no time they'd have next to nothing because of the extreme flood damage and lack of work. The thought of becoming destitute mortified him! His decision had to be right, or he'd fail his family and himself. He walked on. Soon, he found himself in front of what was left of Ma and Pa's small brownstone. The front door frame was swollen from the rain. He used the entire force of his body on the door to get inside.

Some of the flood water had receded, but the house was still under eighteen inches of filthy water, the sodden furniture still floating. Miraculously, he found an undamaged family photo on a high shelf, and he was grateful that it had been spared. He reached up to take it along with him.

Behind the photo was the sugar bowl.

He had forgotten about the sugar bowl! Ma and Pa always stashed money there. For years, they put away any extra pennies or dollars they had for the unexpected. Both of his parents were natural-born worriers, so he knew that they wouldn't have touched it. Joseph lifted the lid and looked inside, and a gasp escaped his lips. Before he left the house, he said goodbye to Ma and Pa and offered a little prayer. He had the photo and the sugar bowl, and most importantly, he had his answer.

Joseph walked back to Freddie and Emma, clear in his decision. "Yes, Freddie. We'll do it. We will leave here." Then silent tears came to everyone as they processed the extreme impact of what had happened and what was yet to come.

PREP STAGE: Freddie's Plan

The seriousness of the situation was palpable. Freddie became laser focused. "OK then. The first step of this journey starts with the bank. You'll need funds to prepare for the journey as well as to acquire those horses and ranches. Getting your Hard Wallet ranch is the final step, the last thing we do. Don't worry. Maverick and I will accompany you and together, we will give you a clear plan."

Emma was starting to feel anxious. This was actually going to happen! She asked Freddie, "Do y'all know a good location for our Hard Wallet ranch?"

"Yes," said Freddie. "I definitely do. It's right by me. But, as I said, that happens in the final step. The best way to secure the best ranches for you is to proceed one step at a time. Better not to rush. This approach will ensure that you get the right horses and ranches for your future operations. Before you take your herd of horses to your Hard Wallet ranch, you'll need to find a working ranch in the Soft Wallet Ranch Territory closer to the second auction house that's located halfway through the frontier. That ranch is important because that's where you'll prepare to do most of your trading for your hard wallet ranch horses."

Joseph wasn't following.

"Freddie, couldn't we just settle into a Soft Wallet ranch then? You say that it's easier to reach and that we'll be setting up a nice farm and ranch there. We don't need much else."

Freddie explained, "Joseph, you'll have a ranch in both territories, next to mine. You want both. Having only the one ranch puts you at too much risk of losing everything. Ranches in both territories have challenges and benefits. The Soft Wallet ranches are the easiest to reach, but they're the bandits' prime target because they're right along the Blockchain Trail. The Hard Wallet ranches are remote, much harder to reach, but safer from potential attacks.

"The ranchers and farmers in the Soft Wallet Ranch Territory have lost more than their share of crops and livestock. We don't keep our best horses there for very long. The Soft Wallet ranch is more for passing through and quick rests. The horses I keep at my Soft Wallet ranch are not my best. They're mostly for quick horse trading and swapping at the auction. So, if you tell me that you're ready to start, I'll have Maverick come to the boardinghouse, and we will talk you through each step."

Freddie continued. "Cousins, when you review the map, you'll see Soft Wallet Ranch Territory extends for miles into the middle of the frontier, where the second auction house is also situated. It's there that you'll be trading a good amount of your trail horses for the more valuable BTC horses that you'll keep at your own Hard Wallet Ranch. Mainly, I want you to focus on staying with me through each step. We'll show you the plan. Between the plan and the map, you'll know exactly what will take place at each step. If you still don't quite understand why you want a ranch in each territory, it will become clear later. I promise."

Emma and Joseph were catching on. Freddie could tell.

"We're going to help you at each juncture, you have my word."

They were exhausted and needed to rest now. They agreed to start the next morning. Freddie continued. "I'll introduce you to Maverick at noon tomorrow. Before he joins us, we'll go to the bank."

STAGE ONE: Get Ready: Mindset, Money, and Mapping

Going to the Bank

The next morning, Freddie accompanied Joseph and Emma to the bank. In addition to the sugar bowl money, the bank manager helped them pull out the funds they would need for it all. All in, they had enough to fill three different sacks and a small chest with coins. They were ready. Having helped them at the bank, Freddie knew what they had to work with. With $8,000 in total, Freddie would have them spend no more than $6,000, leaving $2,000 for incidentals and the unforeseen.

- Going to the Bank
- Organizing the Budget
- Review the Steps
- Prep for the Auction House
- Review the Map

Organizing the Budget

Freddie gave them their budget.

EXPENSES	
Equipment including a covered wagon and supplies	$350
Weapons and ammunition	$100
The Soft Wallet Ranch with a barn, a house, and corrals	$750
Funds for the trail	$150
The Hard Wallet Ranch	$250
Outfitting the Ranch	$1850
Total cost	$3450
Note: What remained for the Auction House was $2550.	

Now, for a Commercial Break

(Or, for you frontier fans, taking a quick break at High Noon)

Dear Reader,
Any new ideas and concepts can seem complicated at first. Freddie's seven-stage process simplifies the complex world of horse trading for her cousins (and crypto trading for you in Part 2). As we continue, my intention for this tall tale is to deepen your understanding of crypto and blockchain through the FOMOs' adventure into their new frontier. They're story prepares you for your journey that comes later. Before you embark into the world of crypto, I mean, horse trading, here are a few facts you need to know.

- **crypto exchanges = auction houses**
- **cryptocurrencies = horses**
- **Freddie's way = her strategy to carefully investing in these new frontiers.**

Freddie's bidding strategy for the FOMOs involves starting with the top-ranked horses available for auction. For you as beginners, that equates to acquiring coins that are among the most established cryptocurrency coins or tokens. THE FOMO's ULTIMATE GOAL: To secure a Hard Wallet ranch and fill it with BTC (Bitcoin) horses.

THE SEVEN STAGE PROCESS:

Stage One: Get Ready: Mindset, Money, and Mapping
Prepare to fund equipment, ranches, and horses.

Stage Two: Shopping for Assets
Buy the equipment, the wagon, and the horses for the trail.

Stage Three: Perils of the Journey
Fortify security.

Stage Four: Get The Soft Wallet Ranch
Locate a good Soft Wallet ranch to keep the Alt horses and Tether ponies that are best for swapping and trading.

Stage Five: Time to Trade
The FOMOs trade up for BTC horses for their Hard Wallet ranch.

Stage Six: Don't Get Misdirected!
Minimize and avoid the dangers and pitfalls of the trail.

Stage Seven: Safe at Home
Secure the Hard Wallet Ranch for the BTC horses.

Note: With so many crypto coins and tokens, it can be challenging to keep them straight. Because of that, I've simplified the story by referencing only a handful of coin examples. "BTC horses" loosely refers to Bitcoin, "ETH horses" refers to Ethereum, and "Tether ponies" speaks to the stablecoin, Tether (USDT). Any other coins fall under the categories of Alt horses, bangtails, bucking broncos, and Pump 'n Dumps. I've taken poetic license by mixing metaphors a bit, but not to worry, you'll get it.

Below are photos of a few of the horses the FOMOs will get at auction. The images below show definitions used in the story and their equivalent in the world of crypto. As the FOMOs learn to become seasoned horse traders, you'll learn about trading crypto.

PART ONE: THE STORY OF THE FOMOS

AUCTION HOUSES
CRYPTO EXCHANGES

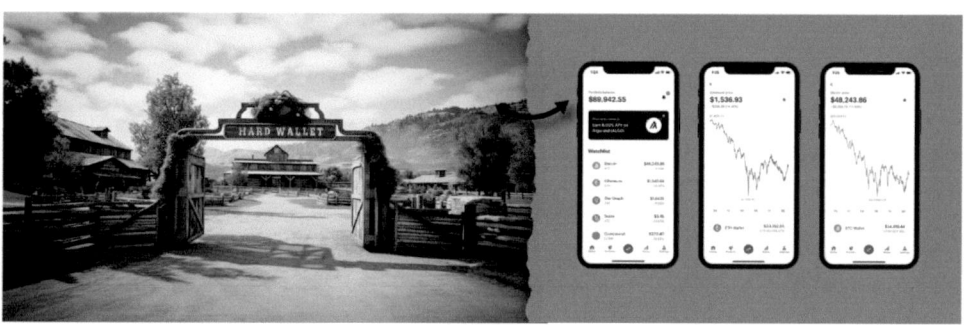

THE RANCH
CRYPTO WALLET

HORSES
CRYPTO COINS

FOMO Terms	Crypto Terms
Auction House Fees	Gas fees at crypto exchanges
The Frontier	The crypto economy. The decentralized financial (DeFi) economic system
Hard Wallet Ranch	Off-line wallet for crypto storage (more secure)
Soft Wallet Ranch	On-line wallet for holding crypto (many are apps)
BTC Horse	Bitcoin (BTC)
ETH Horse	Ethereum. Which is decentralized digital money (ETH)
Tether Ponies	Stablecoins - a digital currency that is pegged to a "stable" reserve asset like the U.S. dollar or gold.
New Bucking Broncos	Like penny stocks. These are coins that are new, untested and/or positioned for astronomical gains or losses.
Alt Horses	Altcoins - refers to a group of cryptocurrencies. Ultimately all the cryptocurrencies other than Bitcoin and traditional fiat money.

***Auction house fees are like gas fees**. A gas fee is a transaction fee on the Ethereum blockchain network. According to Ethereum's developer pages, gas fees are "the fuel that allows the Ethereum network to operate, in the same way that a car needs gasoline to run." Other cryptocurrencies may simply call these transaction fees, miner fees, or something similar.

Back from the Break: Time to Meet Maverick...

After the bank, they returned to the boardinghouse. Maverick had already arrived and was awaiting them on the porch. Upon entering the house, Maverick removed his cowboy hat to show his respect. Standing an imposing six feet, four inches without a hat, he was more than tall! Emma could sense that he was dangerous. Feeling a quick shiver down her spine, she knew that one wrong move could cost you your life with this one. She felt a quick shiver down her spine. He looked very much like a maverick, being both mysterious and impossible to overlook. But he also inspired trust. Junior took to him immediately.

They all made their way to the parlor.

"Nice to make your acquaintance. Call me Maverick. And you are…?"

Joseph stepped forward to greet him. "I'm Joseph. Nice to meet you. This is the Mrs., Emma, and our boy, Junior. I'm Freddie's cousin."

Maverick nodded to both Emma and Junior. He then looked straight at Joseph as he talked to the group. "Listen up, I'm the best guide on the Blockchain Trail. I've crossed it more times than I can count. I'll do my part to keep you safe. I know Freddie's plan for getting those ranches for you. It will work. We just need to follow it. What we can't account for are the dangers of the frontier. That's why Freddie has me here."

Review the Stages

After a few more niceties, it was now time to review the stages of the journey. Freddie took the afternoon to review them with her cousins.

Hopefully, dear reader, they now look familiar.

Prep Stage: Freddie's Plan
Stage One: Get Ready: Mindset, Money, and Mapping
Stage Two: Shopping for Assets
Stage Three: Perils of the Journey
Stage Four: Get The Soft Wallet Ranch
Stage Five: Time to Trade
Stage Six: Don't Get Misdirected!
Stage Seven: Safe at Home

Freddie's plan wasn't the biggest challenge. When it came to traveling across the frontier, her cousins were novices, wet behind the ears. Maverick reminded her that small victories along the way would keep them focused on the end goal and less on the potential dangers that lay ahead. Horse husbandry was in Emma's blood, so Freddie knew that Emma would naturally be drawn to the best horses. The most coveted and highly sought-after horses were the BTC horse breed, which also made them the most expensive and in the shortest supply. Because their budget was somewhat modest, at the first auction house they'd need to bid for the less costly Alt horse breeds, then, with time, as they mastered how to exchange and trade up, they would soon be ready to acquire the BTC horses as they reached the fifth stage of the journey.

Prep for the Auction House

Freddie created another checklist, showing all they'd need to buy from the auction house and the feed store and handed them the list.

"Here y'all go. You'll need a frontier wagon, your supplies, everything from saddles to chaps, blankets, foodstuffs, hats, boots, weapons, and grain for the horses. Tomorrow, Maverick and I will take you to the city's biggest auction house that sells the horses, the Tether ponies, and the tack. The feed store is there too."

This was their list...

- A frontier wagon
- Tack and supplies
- Foodstuffs and cooking equipment
- Hats, boots, and trail clothes
- A Pigeon Phone for the frontier territories
- Double-barreled guns and pistols
- ETH horses to pull the wagon
- Alt horses and Tether ponies for trading

The list included all they would need to get onto the trail. For the first part of the trek, they would need horses with endurance and strength enough to pull the wagon. Although there were always loads of breeds being traded at the auction house, to start, they only needed three horse breeds: Tether ponies (like the stablecoin), ETH horses (like Ethereum), and Alt horses (like altcoins).

With their years of experience, Freddie and Maverick now had an ironclad approach to horse trading and bidding. Freddie went into detail about what they would buy now.

"Y'all, to get from the city's border, through the Outpost, and onto Soft Wallet Ranch Territory, we ranchers want horses with strength and stamina. We need some Tether ponies for the trail, but mostly, you will want to keep a handful of Tether ponies "on credit" with the auction houses. Tether ponies are like a dollar bill. They don't change their value much and we ranchers like to exchange Tether ponies for other horses at the auction house. Having Tether ponies on credit is better for bidding than just using dollars." Then Maverick added, "Joseph, having 'pony' credit on account at both auction houses also means that we don't need to drive all those Tether ponies across the frontier. That makes riding the trail much easier."

Joseph thought that maybe having Tether ponies "on credit" at the auction house was foolhardy. "No, Joseph," Maverick answered. "The auction houses prefer that so the Tether ponies don't get tuckered out from being on the trail. They keep a record of the number of Tether ponies on your account. Freddie and I have hundreds of Tether ponies on credit for trading."

"Ah," Joseph replied with quiet relief. "I understand."

The ETH horses were the most robust, strong as bulls, and the best breed to pull wagons across the frontier. They could endure the worst of conditions, unlike the sickly pump 'n dump horses and the skiddish bangtail mustangs (like unreliable crypto coins). On the frontier, pioneers pulling wagons and moving their herds across the trail needed a good number of ETH horses to keep those wagons moving.

The Alt horses were the breeds of choice for swapping, trading, and bartering and had more stamina than Tether ponies. Sometimes, their value would go up, especially if they happened to be favored or popular. It was common that pioneers would trade with one another on the trail, and they'd rather trade an Alt horse than an ETH horse any day, because it was the ETH horses that pulled the wagons. Having unhealthy ETH horses would put any pioneer on the frontier in harm's way, leaving those horses vulnerable to predators, like bears. Emma wanted those BTC horses right away. Freddie reminded Emma that they would bid for BTC horses at the second auction house, once they had set up their Soft Wallet ranch. Freddie and Emma reviewed the list one final time for stage one.

- **Going to the Bank**
- **Organizing the Budget**
- **Review the Steps**
- **Prep for the Auction House**
- **Review the Map**

Freddie instructed the FOMOs to buy horses from the Top Five Horses List, keeping in mind they needed Tether ponies for trading and ETH and Alt horses for the trail. She gave them an exact list of what to bid on at auction:

AUCTION LIST

80 Tether ponies (stablecoin breed) toput on credit @ $10 each	$800
25 Tether ponies for trail (to have at the Soft Wallet Ranch)	$250
10 ETH horses to pull the wagon and to exchange @ $75 each	$750
15 Altcoin horses to trade @ $50 each	$750
BTC horses	Auction house 2
Additional horses @ $25 each	Auction house 2
0 NFT horses	Not reliable
Auction house fees (gas fees)	Rates fluctuate

After some consideration, Joseph and Emma knew that they wanted at least ten BTC horses for their Hard Wallet ranch. They understood that would happen later. For now, Freddie recommended horse picks that carried a bit more risk, but it was the most prudent way for them to begin as new ranchers. Learning to become better traders using the Alt horses and Tether ponies would get them closer to their goal of buying those BTC horses at the second auction house. If Freddie was right, then this plan would very quickly get their proverbial saddles broken in.

Maverick took the lead.

"Listen, y'all. I imagine your brains are somewhat foggy right about now. Rest assured, I'll prepare you for what's coming. I'm sure you'd like to know all the twists and turns before we go, but that's impossible. What's important is that we work together, stay vigilant, and keep close. Freddie's horse-buying plan will keep you from getting swindled."

"When we arrive at the auction house, you'll get your bidding number, then we'll inspect the horses. We'll get your tack, supplies, your wagon, and anything else you'll need at the feed store before the bidding starts."

Joseph had never been to an auction house before. As was his way, he wanted to know more. "Maverick, what makes for a good auction house that you can trust?"

Maverick gave his criteria while the FOMOs listened closely.

Maverick's Seven Criteria for an Auction House

	Auction House	Crypto Exchange
Criteria 1	The auction house's longevity	How established and active is the exchange?
Criteria 2	Stellar horse inventory	What cryptocurrencies does the exchange platform feature? Do they have the more established cryptocurrencies??
Criteria 3	How secure and safe it is. Have they had bandit attacks? Did the auction house protect the ranchers' purchases?	Has the exchange ever been hacked? Are there complaints about the exchange? Search to find out.
Criteria 4	Is the auction house respected by the community?	Is it well-funded? Look at their trading volume and online portfolio. How is customer support?
Criteria 5	Does it work with more seasoned ranchers?	Does the exchange offer opportunities and lower fees for more seasoned traders?
Criteria 6	Can you take your horses right after you've placed your bids or is there a holding period?	Does the exchange have a transfer delay for your crypto? Do they have security holds on funds and trades?
Criteria 7	How do they surpass their competitors?	Are there specific benefits on that exchange?

Dear Reader,

Cryptocurrency exchanges have been set up in many countries. In the United States, digital asset investors new to cryptocurrency often use the Coinbase platform which is publicly traded on NASDAQ. Being a publicly traded company is the exception, not the rule. Exchanges are not closely monitored or regulated, so researching their viability for your needs is critical.

Freddie had plenty more to say about getting prepared.

"Y'all, on the trail, you'll be making stops for resupplying, trading, and watering the horses at the Outpost. I'll take my leave now and will be waiting for you in the Soft Wallet Ranch Territory. I want to get a jump start on finding you some land there. Once you get your horses and supplies, you'll leave the city and head to the Outpost, which will take a few days. It's there that your will find the Blockchain Trail trailhead to enter the frontier. After the Outpost, Maverick will guide you to the Soft Wallet Ranch Territory. That's where we'll meet up again."

"There's a ranch for sale near me with a corral big enough for your first herd of horses. On the trail, you'll likely be trading those Tether ponies and Alt horses. Maverick will make sure they're good trades. With any luck, you'll have grown your herd! And when you arrive, we can always do more trading before we continue the next leg of the journey to the second auction house."

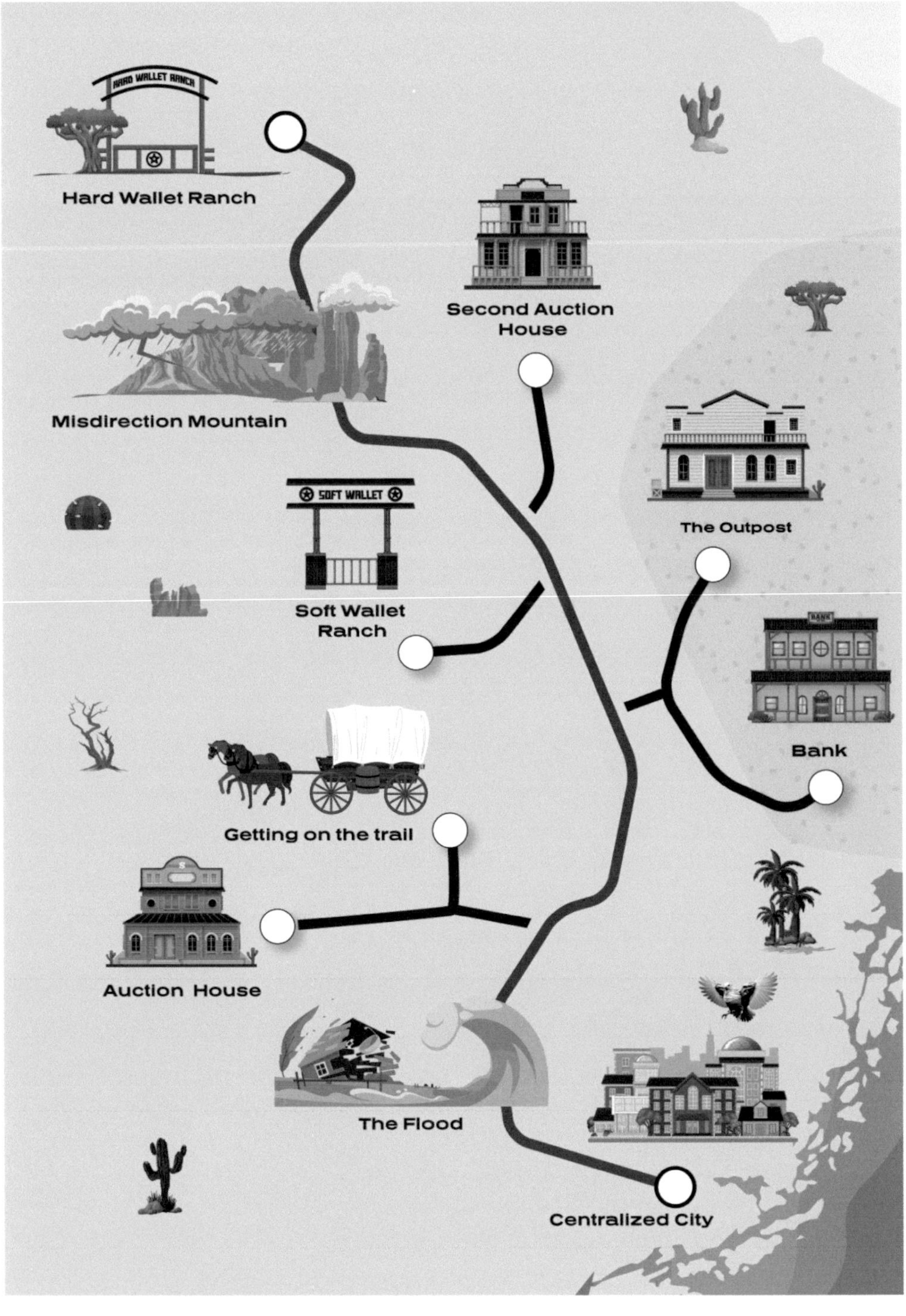

THE BLOCKCHAIN TRAIL

Review the Map

It was time to review the route. This was Maverick's domain. He pulled out a giant map, placing it flat on the table, and began to talk them through each milestone. Junior was more excited than a Mexican jumping bean! Feeling suddenly bittersweet, he pulled out the special compass that Ma and Pa had given him for his birthday. He carefully placed it on the map. "Mama, Papa, this map is amazing! Let me figure out which way is north."

"Junior," Maverick said, "can you write?"

"Yes, I can!" Junior answered.

"Well, take this pencil," said Maverick. "Highlight our stops on the map as I tell you where we're going."

"OK, Maverick. Thank you!"

"Junior, you can be in charge of the map. That's a big job. You'll need to keep it safe and dry in your saddlebag. Can you do that?"

"Yes, Maverick. I'll do it!" Maverick turned the map toward Junior, looking him straight in the eyes so he fully understood the weight of his task.

As he talked them through each stage, stop, and milestone, Junior noted the distances on the map. The most they could travel each day was about twenty miles. Maverick looked back at Junior. "Junior, you'll keep us on our route with the map, the Pigeon Phone, and your compass. If you see that we have gone off the trail, tell me fast. The Pigeon Phone maps the route, but they don't always work right. Sometimes lightning storms fiddle with their settings. So, you're going to need to double-check each thing separately and make sure they are all taking us in the same direction. If the compass and Pigeon Phones have different indicators, then we're lost. And that's dangerous. Understand?"

"Yes, sir," said Junior. He knew this was serious.

"I'm giving each of you the latest Pigeon Phone 2.0, made for the frontier. Most pioneers have never even heard of them because I invented them myself. There are only a handful of them around. This version lets you call anyone, anywhere, anytime on the frontier and inside Centralized City. And it has a built-in compass to tell you exactly where you are. Whatever you do, keep them safe! This is the only one each of you will get."

Presenting the latest Pigeon Phone 2.0, invented for the frontier.

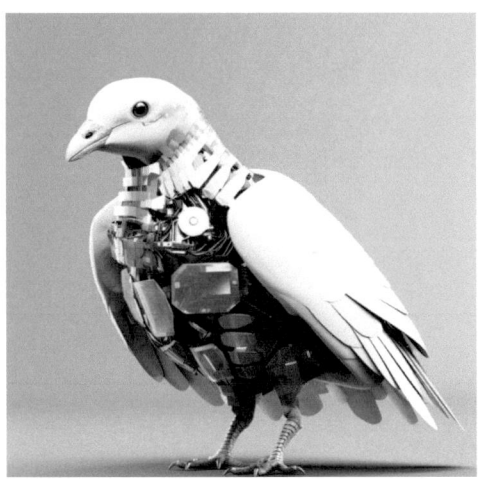

The day was tiring, long and filled with details, but Maverick and Freddie could see that the FOMOs were ready. Freddie got quiet for a moment. Her heart was filled with both love and trepidation, to be true. She had seen the best and worst of the trail and would do all she could to ease their way.

STEP TWO: Shopping for Assets

Prep Stage: Freddie's Plan
Stage One: Get Ready: Mindset, Money, and Mapping.
Stage Two: Shopping for Assets
Stage Three: Perils of the Journey
Stage Four: Get The Soft Wallet Ranch
Stage Five: Time to Trade
Stage Six: Don't Get Misdirected!
Stage Seven: Safe at Home

The auction house had its own set of actions.

- Selecting the Auction House
- Getting an Account
- Picking Horses
- Buying

Selecting Your Auction House and Getting an Account

The next morning, they all met in front of the auction house. The front gates were enormous! The auction house had ceilings as high as a Catholic church! Joseph couldn't help but be taken in by it all as he absorbed the sights, smells, and sounds of the place. It was time to head in. Maverick hurried them along. "No time to waste. Let's get those bidding numbers!"

They handed the cashier a pouch of coins as their deposit, receiving their bidding paddles in return. Hanging high for all to see was a large electronic banner, a marquee that listed the Top Five Horses which included the top-traded breeds that Freddie wanted them to bid on. It displayed the horse breeds, the starting bid price, what the breed was used for, and how they ranked.

Picking Horses

Maverick and Freddie reminded the FOMOs what they were there to accomplish. "Y'all know what you're bidding on—only horse breeds in the Top Five. For ETH horses, we want animals that already have good coats for winter. We'll make sure that you only bid on the healthiest and best horses at the right price."

The stables were full of more horse breeds and Tether ponies than they could count! Maverick explained what to look for when inspecting horses at auction. The first round of bidding would be mostly for horses that were good for the trail and valuable for trading with other pioneers.

"Make sure you walk all the way around the animal and look at it from hoof to ears. They need to be healthy." This auction house was good at keeping out bad horses. Still, they needed to understand how to recognize a good one.

Horses	Crypto
Does the horse have healthy teeth?	Does cryptocurrency have a reliable and secure technological foundation?
Is the animal calm or fearful? (that may tell you how the horse has been treated)	Is cryptocurrency stable?
Does it have a good winter undercoat?	Is cryptocurrency financially healthy?
Is it strong enough for the trail?	Does the cryptocurrency have a useful purpose or benefit? Does it solve real-world problems?

After they walked the stables, they headed to the feed store and bought what they needed from their list. In no time, the auction bell rang.

"Let's go now and make our bids," said Emma.

The FOMOs' Bidding Plan

80 Tether ponies (stablecoin breed) to put on credit @ $10 each	$800
25 Tether ponies for trail (to have at the Soft Wallet Ranch)	$250
10 ETH horses to pull the wagon and to exchange @ $75 each	$750
15 Altcoin horses to trade @ $50 each	$750
BTC horses	Auction house 2
Additional horses @ $25 each	Auction house 2
0 NFT horses	Not reliable
Auction house fees (gas fees)	Rates fluctuate

The strategist in Emma had wanted to learn the best approach for timing their bids. Maverick counseled her. "Emma, it's good to buy on the dip, when the prices are low. Never good to buy when there's a wild run-up on the prices (in crypto-speak, that is called euphoria). We don't want to act like crazed chickens being chased by a fox! Prices can change fast here. Better to first take note of the horse's health, then its temperament, and then the price. You'll bid to get your horses at the lowest prices possible. But today is about getting the best horses for the difficult terrain."

"Maverick, look up. What's that big sign for?" Junior asked.

PART ONE: THE STORY OF THE FOMOS   79

Breed	Symbol	Breeder	Starting Bid	Personality	Utility of Horse	Volume of Horses Trading
Bitcoin Horse	BTC	BTC Ranch	$150	Calm and steady	Breeding, hold value	15
Ethereum Horse	ETH	ETH Ranch	$75	Warm-blooded and strong	Pulling the wagon	50
Tether Pony	USDT	Tether Ranch	$10	Social	Hold for exchanging	750
Solana Horse	DRAFT	LTC Ranch	$50	Interested	Hauling	100
Algorand Horse	QTR	Algo Horse Ranch	$75	Patient, calm, intelligent	Trail riding	75
Meme Horse	MEME	Mustang Ranch	$25	Erratic, fearful, can be powerful	Risky	200

"Junior, that's the marquee that lists the Top Five Horses. It shows the bidders the breed, the lineage, and the breeder's ranch. Seasoned ranchers look for the name of the ranch that's bred the horses they want. Before you bid, you want to make sure that they have done a good job caring for their animals.

"We want to get horses from respectable ranchers. Some scallywags make a quick-buck swindling newbie ranchers by over-breeding pump 'n dump horses, then selling them as young bucking broncos. Woe to anyone that falls prey to those critters.

"Next, you want to understand why the horse is for sale and figure out if it's been bought and sold before. Could mean there's a problem we can't see. Remember, on the frontier, anything goes. Pump 'n dump horses can also be mixed breeds and are not always easy to spot. Those creatures are good for nothing and will empty your pockets! Some of the most beautiful horses are useless! They are pretty to look at but have no substance—none of the capabilities a horse needs. They just aren't sturdy or practical. Of course, you check their teeth, their hooves, and how they're shoed. You also want to confirm their temperament and if the horse is broken in. Look in that stall over here at the ETH horse gelding. Let's go in and I'll show you what I look for."

Seeing how interested Junior was in trading, Emma pulled him aside. "I'm giving you a small allowance. Do with it what you want—but don't forget what Maverick has taught you." Excited, and with dollar signs in his eyes, Junior ran off and scouted all the horses and ponies at the auction house, not really giving much mind to Maverick's warnings.

> **SIDE NOTE**
>
> "Pump and dump" scams, also termed as "rug pulls," represent a deceptive practice common in the cryptocurrency realm. These manipulative schemes involve scammers spreading misleading news about a particular cryptocurrency project to artificially inflate its value. Subsequently, when a significant number of retail investors get drawn into purchasing the coin, the fraudsters sell off their holdings (equivalent to "pulling the rug"). This results in considerable profits for the fraudsters, while the unsuspecting investors bear the brunt of the financial loss as the value of the coin drastically plummets.[3]

The ETH horse gelding stood fifteen hands high and had a nice, thick coat. Maverick gave it a piece of carrot so he could inspect its teeth while it chewed. He circled the horse a few times, feeling for inconspicuous lumps and slight joint protrusions. He watched it walk around the stall as he tried to spot any obvious issues. The horse seemed well-fed, had a strong demeanor, held its head and tail high, and had lungs that sounded strong. It also didn't look too old, or sick. When he inspected the hooves, he saw that the horse had been newly shoed. Based on the color of its teeth, he figured its age at about five years, a good age for a horse!

Maverick had a few more tricks up his sleeve. "Joseph, watch the veteran ranchers. Ask them about what they're seeing at auction today and what they're looking for. You'll learn something. When you're beginning, don't do your bidding alone."

---

[3] Definitions generated or vetted by ChatGPT, 2023, OpenAI, https://chat.openai.com. Rewritten for style and content.

Then, puffing up like a giant green feathered peacock, he said, "Can you see why having your own maverick can save your saddles? Going it alone is like riding an unbroken mustang backward and naked!"

Joseph had a grapefruit-sized pit in his stomach. He pulled Emma to the side. "Darlin', I think we might be going too fast with that horse list. Freddie's saying to get over one hundred Tether ponies? I think we should get fewer horses since we're just starting. Getting all those horses across the trail to the Soft Wallet ranch won't be easy!"

No stranger to figuring out odds, Emma could see that without buying what Freddie recommended, it would be impossible to trade successfully as they traveled. They'd never make enough to buy those BTC horses. Emma saw Freddie's logic. "Joseph, I say we take more risk while we are closer to the city, with those Tether ponies and Alt horses. I know we could lose money, get robbed, or have horses collapse on the trail, but we'll make nothing if we don't follow her lead. Then the risk we've taken would have been for nothing. I'm worried about things going wrong and losing too, but if we don't try Freddie's way, we definitely won't win. Not right now anyway."

Dear Reader,

What do you think would be best for the FOMOs to do? Should they start more slowly? What would you do? Before you start investing in crypto or anything at all really, you want a clear strategy that begins with understanding your investment risk tolerance and your investment time horizons. Let's find out where you stand. Use this link to find out what investor type you are!

www.TamingCryptoBook.com/Investor

After they placed their bids, Maverick asked an important question. "Joseph, Emma, why do you want to be ranchers now? You'll get your ranches. But when you think about working them, what do you see in your mind's eye? Will you mostly breed? Or do you want to farm or mine? What about cattle and oxen? My own ranch got much bigger after I could see it in my mind. Let's talk about your new ranches and what you'll do with them."

Freddie could see their eyes turn into saucers just by hearing the questions. She intervened. "Joseph, while y'all take to the trail, you'll have plenty of time to figure that out. The clearer you are, the more we can help you. I'm heading out now with my new horses and a few of my horsemen. But I'll have a few of my horse hands travel with you and help with your herd. And if there's trouble ahead, we'll find it before it finds you."

She hugged her cousins. "See y'all out on the frontier! I love you!" Then Freddie took her leave.

Dear Reader,
I ask the same of you. What would compel you to step into crypto? Every realized outcome begins with a vision. What are your financial interests and goals? Do you have a vision yet for your financial present and future? Do you know what your next steps might be?

STAGE THREE: Perils of the Journey

The New Frontier: Soft Wallet Ranch Territory
This territory sits west of Centralized City and officially starts at the Outpost.

> **Stage One:** Get Ready: Mindset, Money, and Mapping
> **Stage Two:** Shopping for Assets
> **Stage Three: Perils of the Journey**
> **Stage Four:** Get Your Soft Wallet Ranch
> **Stage Five:** Time to Trade
> **Stage Six:** Don't Get Misdirected!
> **Stage Seven:** Safe at Home

The FOMOs won their bids for the exact number of horses that Freddie had recommended. With their new horses and frontier wagons, they were ready to leave the city and head toward Freddie's Soft Wallet ranch, but the long distance would require them to stop at the Outpost for more supplies. Reviewing their new, four-legged acquisitions, one animal really stuck out, a brightly colored unicorn pony. Baffled, Maverick, Emma, and Joseph scratch their heads while Junior stood there beaming with pride. They all turned their attention to him. "Isn't it pretty? I'm calling it Gumdrop!"

Realizing what had happened, Emma immediately realized that she'd made a mistake by not directly overseeing Junior's first bid and purchase. Walking around Gumdrop, Maverick shook his head while doing his best to hide his disappointment. "Young'uns just don't listen," he muttered under his breath, then walked away.. Junior, in the meantime, was excited to have such a beautiful horse that was his and his alone.

Having no time to waste, Maverick shook off his disapproval, and returned to the group briefing them in detail about the perils of the trail, not because he was a negative sort, but because the territories had taught him as such.

Dangers on the Blockchain Trail included:

- They could lose their way or be led astray.
- They could be robbed.
- The horses could be injured from extreme weather conditions (like crypto winters can do to coins!).

- Veteran ranchers and breeders could mess with horse prices (which also happens when crypto whales flex their muscles in the crypto markets).
- They could fall prey to deceitful pump 'n dump horse breeders.
- The city's governing council could impose new regulations on the territories that could turn back the progress for the early pioneers that risked everything to get a solid financial foothold while the frontier was still untamed.

SIDE NOTE

"Cryptocurrency whales" (or "crypto whales" for short) are individuals or entities that own large quantities of a specific cryptocurrency, so much so that they can move crypto prices quickly by trading substantial amounts of coins and tokens. "Crypto winters" are prolonged periods of pricing weakness in the cryptocurrency market. When markets face a crypto winter, retail investors tend to get spooked, and market chaos often times ensues.[4]

The Blockchain Trail had a bit of everything you'd rather not deal with, like bandits, rug pullers, conniving hackers, crypto-jackers, and other bad actors. The FOMOs would need to stay laser-focused on their goals and small victories, not allowing the risks of the trail to deter them. As the sun rose, Maverick yelled out, "Let's head 'em up and move 'em out!" Joseph

[4] *Definitions generated or vetted by ChatGPT, 2023, OpenAI, https://chat.openai.com. Rewritten for style and content.*

cracked the whip over the heads of the ETH horses pulling the frontier wagon as the horse hands rode behind the herd.

The milestone of this first leg of the trail was reaching the Outpost, the border town between the Centralized City settlement and the Soft Wallet Ranch Territory. That would take a few travel days. Aside from its huge livery stable, the Outpost was equally famous for its great card-playing saloons, which was music to Emma's ears, since she was quite the card shark. But the Outpost had a very rough-and-tumble side too, hosting more than a few unpleasant skirmishes between the city settlers and the aspiring ranchers beginning their trek into the Soft Wallet Ranch Territory.

The frontier's open skies took their breath away. All their senses were firing with so many sights and sounds they had never before experienced. Aside from the sheer expanse of the landscape, the FOMOs encountered some peculiar types of horses they'd never seen. One such breed was the NFT horses, like Junior's unicorn pony, which looked more like horses of the gods than beasts of burden. Each NFT horse was known to have its own unique personality. Which of these horses would make it across the frontier, only time would tell, but they were always a sight to behold.

On their second night under the dark sky, the FOMOs camped near other pioneers. Staying close to his unicorn, Junior tended to Gumdrop's every need, carefully brushing its tri-colored mane, and gently stroking its forehead. Emma's heart warmed as she watched her son care for the animal.

Knowing there was safety in numbers, they quickly combined with other traveling pioneers, sharing their large campfire. This other group was heading north toward the Metaverse Territory, a region the FOMOs hadn't heard of before. Maverick explained, "That's due north, beyond the Hard Wallet Ranch Territory. I haven't ventured into those parts yet."[5]

Junior's curiosity got the best of him. "Why not, Maverick?"

"Because, Junior, I like guiding pioneer families like yours that need help finding ranches in the lower territories. There are other guides who trek that upper north territory with their eyes closed."

Each day they learned more from others they met along the trail. They heard about ranchers settling into both the Soft Wallet and Hard Wallet Ranch Territories. They also heard about endless different horse breeds. Some showed impressive rigor, while other breeds dropped like flies.

They reached the Outpost on the fifth day, feeling dusty, sore, and tired. Hungry for a hot meal, the FOMOs, Maverick, and the horsemen rode up to the livery stable with the horses in search of food. The stable keepers took the horses to feed and water them. Maverick was satisfied that the horses were holding strong so far.

When they entered the Outpost, some pioneers leaving town told them about a posse of crypto-jacking outlaws roaming the border. Freddie had anticipated this and found them a safe camping spot by a creek for the night. Following their meals, Maverick led the FOMOs and the other pioneers to that location, with their horse herds in tow. That spot was secluded and away from the trail, so it took more time to get there, but safety mandated they stay there for the night to avoid trouble. Upon arriving, they circled their wagons before setting up camp.

By now the group of pioneer families and the FOMOs developed a nightly routine. They prepared food, ate together, then huddled around

[5] See resources for info on the Metaverse: tamingcryptobook.com/resources

the fire, trading any new information about horses and Tether ponies, even trading the horses themselves, as well as discussing money-making ideas for their ranches, before heading off to their bedrolls.

One of the other pioneer families had bid for horses at the auction house in the city and won their bids for the Algorand horses. After learning more about other horse types on the trail, the FOMOs realized that adding new Algorand horses to the herd would serve them well. They had horses and ponies to trade, and Maverick agreed that exchanging Tether ponies for Algorand stock was a good swap. It was a quick win for all the pioneers.

While everyone was ready to hit the hay, Emma had a second wind. You see, earlier in town, she'd seen an announcement about a big card tournament with a sizable purse. She had already figured out how many more BTC horses they could buy if she took the winnings. As one of the few lady "fast hands," she was itching to play. Being the sole female card player was nothing new to her. The small pistol that she discreetly tucked away in her garter belt was her insurance that she would be able to leave without too much trouble after she won.

She knew that this tournament would likely be her only chance to play for some time. When they finally found the camping spot, Emma knew what she needed to do. She nonchalantly sidled over to Joseph, gently rubbing his arm. As sly as a minx, she looked up at him, speaking in a soft and sultry voice. "Joseph, darlin', wouldn't it be amazing to have more coins for those BTC horses we're pining for at the next auction house? How's about giving me just a little bit of sugar bowl coin for wagering so I can win that purse in the card tournament?"

"Emma," Joseph said, "we are not gambling the money. We're doing this Freddie's way, which doesn't include playing cards in some joint with a board stretched between two whiskey barrels."

"Yes, dear. I agree," Emma said. "But this ain't no small-time card game in the corner of a saloon. This contest has a good purse! And, of course, we don't want to lose. So, let's you and me go and watch. You know that I only play when I hear Lady Luck's whisperings. If it feels right, I'll wager ten dollars. No more. If I lose, we leave. But I'm feeling lucky. We won't lose. You know I can outplay the best of them. Come on now, Joseph. Trust me on this." Her hand slowly made its way from his arm to his hip. He was starting to feel a little warm under the collar, and he could see the gambler's craze in her eyes. He knew he had to oblige her. So he said, "Sunshine, we'll do it this time, but make it good because this won't happen again." And, for the moment, Emma agreed.

A Tale of Two Clashing Worldviews: The Bar room Brawl That Almost Happened

Making it through the Outpost without a scuffle would always be a crap shoot. The local settlers could be very inhospitable. The pioneers had heard about plenty of run-ins between the local settlers and the ranchers passing through. Maverick was not keen on returning to the Outpost, since they had already set up camp, but he knew that resisting Emma's desire to gamble was no use. He could clearly see that she would let nothing come between her and those cards! He hadn't seen this side of her before. No question her gambler's heart was calling the shots. He accompanied Emma, Joseph, and Junior back to the Outpost and the card room, dismounting the horses by a water trough and tying them to the closest hitching post. They arrived early so Emma could get a quick swig of "liquid courage" at the saloon.

While sitting at the bar ordering shots, a group of shaggy-looking, hat-wearing drunkards sized up the newcomers. Noticing the horses hitched outside, including Junior's rainbow-hued pony, they snickered and laughed at the silly spectacle. Hurt by their scoffing, Junior withdrew behind Maverick. "Don't listen to them," Emma told him. "Junior, sometimes following your heart takes you down a harder road. When it comes to horses, using logic will override what the heart wants. For all we know, Gumdrop could be a strong and healthy horse that's more valuable as it grows. But ponies like Gumdrop are not common; that's why those men are acting so strangely. Never you mind those drunken fools. Just remember what Maverick is teaching us about picking the best horses." Emma then gave them all a stare down.

The barflies worked for the city, handling horse traffic control. Unfortunately, their drunkenness kept them in a brazenly rude state. They were known for writing tickets to pioneers and ranchers who left their horses on the hitching post by the water trough for "too long," issuing additional penalties to any horse that drank "more than its share." One of these horse traffic control yodels hollered at Maverick and the FOMOs, "hey, what are y'all doing there, and what about them horses? They're not sanctioned for these parts anymore! Things are changing, and there are no horses allowed in town without a permit." Maverick and the FOMOs weren't looking for any trouble. They were only there to get a drink and play cards.

Maverick could see that the situation needed to be pacified, so he said, "Gents, we're here to wet our whistles before this lovely lady sits down to play some cards next door. Our apologies for not knowing about this new law. We will be on our way and move the horses from the hitching post to the livery stable."

"That's fine by us," said the drunkest of the group, who was now nose to nose with Maverick and literally swaying on his feet. "We're gonna write you up for violating the new regulation. You got a problem with that?" Maverick knew this could go from bad to worse. "No sir. I'll take the penalty. Do me the favor of stepping back so we can take our leave." The cantankerous drunks looked at one another, ascertaining the kind of opponent Maverick would be if they wrestled him down. They had him outnumbered, but when Maverick stood his tallest wearing his hat, they thought better of testing him, allowing Maverick and the FOMOs to pass. "Leave the bar, and don't do it again. Next time, we won't be so hospitable." The soberest of the drunks wrote the ticket before they all returned to their drinking.

Maverick was quick to put the incident behind him. He wasn't sure about Emma and Joseph, though. "Emma," he said. "If you're still of the mind to play, you and Joseph head over to the card room, and Junior and I will get the horses to the livery stable." Emma was shaken, but not enough to put out that fire for card winnings. They crossed the street, Emma feeling driven by this one chance to boost their coffers. They entered the card room just in time to watch the first few rounds.

Emma had learned to play cards from her father who was a shrewd and agile card shark. She could feel Lady Luck with her that night as she joined the game. The more hands she won, the more she rattled her rivals. They could not abide being outplayed by a lady. It was no matter to Emma. Their agitation only spurred her on to keep winning. Other than horses and family, playing cards was what made life worth living. Emma took the purse that night, turning $10 into $400!

Dear Reader,
As you begin your foray into being as a digital asset investor, you need a bit of a gambler's heart to buy into crypto and blockchain. The technology and the coins are still new. To mitigate the risk, begin with your mad

money. How you will fare depends on several factors. But as unsettled as world economics are right now, anything we do or don't do is gambling at some level, right? How good are you at reading the tells?

Emma tucked her winnings securely into her silk purse, then Maverick quickly escorted the FOMOs to the livery stable. History bears witness to the growing intensity of dissent between the local settlers and the increasing number of new ranchers. The settlers liked being settled and didn't understand why anyone would leave the city for the frontier. But the FOMOs and other pioneers would not be deterred. Determined to become full-time ranchers, there would be no turning back. As they grieved their losses, they were also preparing for a new future. There was no city life to return to, no family there anymore. Their future on the frontier was completely in their hands.

Their next milestone was the Soft Wallet Ranch Territory and Freddie's Soft Wallet ranch. Traveling a few more days on the Blockchain Trail, by Day 3, they were close. Maverick rustled them all up early so they could reach the ranch before the sun hit high noon. Emma was convinced, more than ever, that the frontier would make for a better life.

STAGE FOUR: Get the Soft Wallet

The serpentine trail curved like a slithering rattlesnake. After circling the next bend, they crossed a narrow river, which took some time with the herd. As the wagons and horses made it to the other side of the riverbank, they beheld beautiful farmland that reached to the farthest expanses. Having spent years farming, Emma and Joseph immediately recognized the richness of the land. It was idyllic as both a ranch and a farm. Maverick also took in the vista. He never tired of its beauty. This was life in the Soft Wallet Territory.

Now only a stone's throw from Freddie's ranch, they continued down the trail, coming across a ranch and farm with a beautiful farm stand filled with produce. An older farmer and his missus had been raising crops for a few years, providing produce for pioneers passing through. Emma was immediately drawn to the voluptuous produce while Joseph noticed a sign inviting passersby to shop at the farm stand. The farmer was feeding chickens by the barn as they all approached. "Hey, y'all. Welcome!" the farmer yelled out. "Anything special y'all are looking for today?"

The farm stand was such a sight, filled with a bounty of fresh vegetables and the largest eggs Joseph had ever seen! The chickens were running in all directions and the alfalfa stacked high in the fields made Joseph feel right at home. Their corral was empty but for a rusted "FOR SALE" sign.

"This land is spectacular!" Joseph thought to himself. He wondered what exactly had happened. Horses and cattle were conspicuously missing. While Emma was now lost in the peach section, Joseph asked the farmer about the sign. "Howdy, sir. My name's Joseph and that's the missus, Emma, and our son, Junior. What are y'all selling with that sign?"

"Our ranch," answered the farmer. "The missus and I are getting older now and weren't blessed with children. A while back, crypto-jackers came and robbed us blind. Stole all our horses and cattle, and we don't have the money or the giddy up to start again with more livestock."

Maverick hadn't yet heard about the recent attack. He asked the farmer, "When did that happen?"

The farmer replied, "Wish I could say. I don't rightly know precisely. But the lock on our corral was rusted out and didn't fully shut right. We needed a new lock to secure the corral and just didn't get around to it. A darn shame! We might as well have invited those bandits over for supper! It should have never happened. Now we need to sell everything. The missus isn't talking to me much right now."

Dear Reader,
When soft wallets holding digital assets are hacked, you can probably consider those digital assets gone forever. Because they connect to the internet, the wallets are vulnerable to being hacked. There are steps to take to make your soft wallets less hacker-friendly, but soft wallet security is not an exact science. That's why it's important to invest in a hard wallet for storing digital assets that you are holding and not trading actively. Hard wallets are offline, which adds a layer of security that soft wallets don't have.[6]

After hearing the farmer's tell of his tragic loss, Maverick and Joseph looked at each other, thinking the same thing. Was this man's ranch the Soft Wallet ranch Freddie was thinking about for the FOMOs?

"You have a beautiful ranch here, sir. I'm your neighbor. My name's Maverick. I've admired how well you and the missus have kept up your land and your horses. What a misfortune! Those crypto-jackers are a real scourge! What's your name?" asked Maverick.

---

[6]See resources for information on hard and soft wallets: tamingcryptobook.com/resources

"We're the Smith Family. We've been here for years. We don't want to leave, but it doesn't seem that we have a choice."

Joseph stepped in and said, "Well, my family and I are looking for a ranch in this area and we need someone to run it while we're out trading. How about we buy your ranch and you and the missus keep running it? You keep living in the main house and continue to take care of the farm. We'll be bringing in our horses and would need you to tend to them. What do you say? We can buy the ranch today." Joseph knew that they would be welcome to stay at Freddie's as needed, but they would have a Soft Wallet ranch with a secure corral to call their own. Farmer Smith and Joseph shook hands. It was agreed.

They were eager to tell Freddie about the sheer luck of finding a ranch so quickly! Joseph called Freddie on his Pigeon Phone 2.0 to give her the great news. She was excited beyond words! They finally arrived at the juncture of both Maverick and Freddie's Soft Wallet ranches. The land was fertile, with plenty of grass, good-sized horse barns, and sizable corrals. Their shared pastures gave the horses more space to roam. The FOMOs noticed that the horses in the distance were mostly Tether ponies and Alt horses.

Seeing them approaching, Freddie rode out to help them bring in the herd. "Cousins, I'm so happy to hear about your Soft Wallet ranch! Let's get the horses to pasture then grab some supper." Junior, unable to contain his excitement, burst out, "Cousin Freddie, the ranch is amazing, and it's right close down the way!" Freddie looked approvingly at Maverick.

Dismounting, Joseph took everything in. What a monumental day! They now had their Soft Wallet ranch next to Freddie's. Where they'd stay when they returned to the ranch they'd figure out later, but he was relieved at how seamlessly this milestone had come.

After supper, they gathered in the big room by the fireplace. Freddie was excited about this new development and was ready to explain how she selected the horses for the Soft Wallet ranch as opposed to those for the Hard Wallet ranch.

"Freddie," Joseph said, "the Smiths' ranch has fertile farmland. Riding this trail has been rough. Every time we turn around, there's something to deal with. But farming on the open plains, and growing alfalfa, we know how to do that. Why not settle here for a while? We could use the rest. We could hold off and get that Hard Wallet ranch later. This ranch is set with a large corral and barn! Why not stop now?"

Freddie explained. "Joseph, some pioneers only homestead a Soft Wallet ranch. They don't last long out here. Having a Soft Wallet ranch is good, but not good enough because they are easy targets for bandits. Having only a Soft Wallet ranch puts your herd of horses at greater risk. You never know when the horse thieves, outlaws, or bandits might strike. My approach is having ranches in both territories, but you need to begin with establishing a ranch here first. These ranches are right along the Blockchain Trail, so it's nothing to get the horses in and out for trading. The Hard Wallet ranches are far off the trail, making them much harder to attack. Your more valuable horses are safer there. It's where we keep our BTC and ETH horses to hold and breed."

"Everyone in these parts understands the risks of predators, bandits, and Mother Nature. Horses are more vulnerable to being stolen or attacked by bears. This ranch is a stop, not a final landing place. We don't leave the Tether ponies and horses here long. We take a quick respite, let the horses graze and rest, then head to the next auction house to make trades for our Hard Wallet ranches."

Emma asked Freddie and Maverick, "How do you manage both ranches?"

"We share a ranch manager and ranch hands to tend to the day-to-day when we aren't here. The Smiths will manage your new ranch. For the Hard Wallet ranch, our horsemen can help while you find wranglers of your own."

STAGE FIVE: Time to Trade

Prep Stage: Freddie's Plan
Stage One: Get Ready: Mindset, Money, and Mapping.
Stage Two: Shopping for Assets
Stage Three: Perils of the Journey
Stage Four: Get The Soft Wallet Ranch
Stage Five: Time to Trade
Stage Six: Don't Get Misdirected!
Stage Seven: Safe at Home

Freddie and Maverick witnessed the FOMOs and the Smiths finalize the purchase. The FOMOs received the deed to their new ranch. They immediately replaced that rusted-out lock on the corral and then prepared for the next leg of the journey. Freddie's way was working! Maverick and Freddie helped them to sort out which horses and ponies would stay with the Smiths on their new ranch and which they would take on the trail to the second auction house. They left a few Tether ponies and Altcoin horses behind.

Dear Reader,

Now, the FOMOs have their ranch in the Soft Wallet Ranch Territory. In the crypto world, the soft wallet is a virtual application (app) that lives on your phone and computer. The benefit of a soft wallet is that it's mobile and easy to use for trading and swapping. The downside is that it's vulnerable to hackers because it's connected to the internet. The reality is that most hackers won't target you specifically because it's likely not a highly profitable theft for them. However, in addition to soft wallets, serious crypto investors also have hard wallets to store digital coins offline.

Trading at the Second Auction House

The auction house marquee showed the trading pairs for the day. Emma focused on the horses they could trade for the BTC horses. BTCs were the best horses for breeding, the most expensive, and the most desired. Their Tether ponies on credit would trade for several of the BTC horses. As for the Alt horses, not all of them were approved to trade for the BTCs. They would have to sort out which Alt horses they could exchange for BTC horses.

In cryptocurrency, the term "trading pairs" describes the asset pair being traded (typically one cryptocurrency for another). Consider the "trading pair" ETH/BTC. That trading pair indicates that a trader can trade their ETH for BTC. BTC/ETH shows a trader that they can trade BTC for ETH.

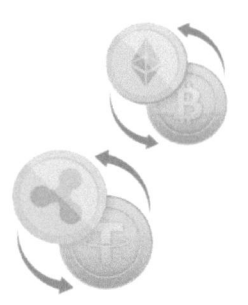

If you transfer U.S. dollars onto an exchange, USD/BTC tells a trader that they can trade U.S. Dollars for BTC (Bitcoin).

Different exchanges allow for different trades or swaps.

The flurry of trading in the morning gave Emma the inkling that the prices for BTCs would go down before the second round of bidding. Maverick wanted them to drive their own wagon when it came to placing their bids, so he stayed in the background. He could see that Emma was masterful at calculating the odds. Come bidding time, the prices had adjusted down enough to get them an extra two BTC horses! The Tether ponies traded for eight more. Twenty ETHs got them five more. That made thirteen BTCs already. She realized that they could also trade twenty of their Alt horses to get another five BTCs. Holy smokes! They'd hoped for ten BTCs and ended up with eighteen! That was a huge windfall! Holding off bidding until the morning trading euphoria had settled down had been the right strategy. When Joseph reconciled the numbers, he recognized how much extra money they had left to acquire additional horses and decided to trade the remaining five Alt horses for a few Memes, a new bucking bronco, and two more Algorand horses. It was a bonanza! Joseph and Emma were ready to celebrate.

Maverick noticed a shift in Emma. She was thinking more like Freddie every day. She still could be impulsive, but her intuition was strong. There was no doubt. Emma was developing into a ranch woman.

They stayed an extra night in town and celebrated like never before. Even the stoic Joseph let loose! They sang old songs with the piano, Emma danced, and Junior hid in the corner thinking that his parents had gone crazy. Feeling like they had conquered the world, they drank a few too many rounds of very strong moonshine! Maverick had one shot but stayed steady because he knew what lay ahead on the trail and had the discipline to stay focused on the end goal. The Misdirection Mountain Pass wasn't very far away, and a traveler never knew what might happen as they traveled that part of the route to Hard Wallet Territory.

Dear Reader,
Don't get sidetracked by big financial windfalls. Getting cocky, misdirected, or distracted can result in losing quickly and badly.

The following morning, they returned to the auction house to gather their new horses. Their herd was a new combination of horses that were headed to the Hard Wallet ranch Territory. They now had:

They now had:
- 10 ETH horses
- 18 BTC horses
- 20 Tether ponies
- 1 Unicorn pony
- 25 Algorand horses
- 5 Solana horses
- 5 Meme horses
- 1 New bucking bronco

Being the first customers to arrive, the cashier, Miss Sarah, for some odd reason, pretended not to recognize them. Averting her glances and speaking in a barely audible voice, she muttered, "I'm sorry, but it looks like I don't have y'all registered from yesterday's auction. What are your names?" The FOMOs weren't prepared for problems right about now. Their hangovers still had them fog-headed. Emma became highly agitated. "What are you talking about?" she impatiently blurted out. "Here's our receipt showing our final bids from yesterday. You don't recognize us? You're the one who gave me my bidding paddle!" Miss Sarah froze.

"Where's your boss?" Joseph demanded, also frustrated. Flustered, Miss Sarah ran to the back to find Big Dale. As he approached the cashier's desk, he recognized Maverick straightaway.

"Mornin', Maverick. Apologies! When I came in this morning, I saw something was off and worried that we'd been attacked by the Black Hat Hacker bandits that have been canvassing the area to steal horses. I was afraid that the ledgers were stolen too since they weren't in their rightful place. Then I noticed that the horses had also been jostled around! I didn't know what the hellfire was going on! Fortunately, my new ledger manager came in at the crack of dawn to audit yesterday's records for any errors on the ledgers. He also re-marked the horses according to our policy. He put yesterday's audited ledger on my desk. I have it here. Miss Sarah, I'll be helping Maverick and his fellow travelers now. You can go."

"Thank you, Big Dale," Sarah said, disappearing to the back of the barn.

The mood changed abruptly, making the combination of excitement and celebration a distant memory. The FOMOs were both off-kilter and fog-headed as they wobbled and swayed in the aftermath of that moonshine. Today's ride would hurt, that was for sure.

Dear Reader,

You never know what can happen on the crypto exchanges. It's a good practice to retain receipts of purchases, bids, or swaps separately from the exchange records, as each exchange keeps records available according to their own policies. There is no industry standard yet for that. Also, savvy traders will remove the digital assets they secure from the exchange when they are not trading or swapping. Everyone using exchanges needs to be cognizant that anything can happen. For example, the exchange can stop or restrict access with no notice. Also, hackers can steal from exchanges, not just from digital asset wallets. Make it a habit to transfer your assets to a secure digital wallet.

FYI: For profit tracking and reporting purposes, you want to track your activity on software outside the exchanges because they do not keep long-term records of your trades. At some point, the IRS in the U.S. might implement policies that tax gains on cryptocurrency transactions and could make tax payments retroactive, so your data needs to be in your control.

STAGE SIX: Don't get Misdirected!

The twists and turns of the trail tested the mettle of everyone there, especially at the higher and colder elevations. They persevered, moving much more slowly in light of the prolonged and unyielding aftereffects of the moonshine. Every night, Junior studied the territory on the map, ensuring they were headed due west and writing down anything new that the map didn't show. He also regularly checked on his Pigeon Phone 2.0 to confirm their location.

Finally, they reached a juncture on the trail that took them northwest through Misdirection Mountain Pass. The Pigeon Phones could not be relied on from that point on, consistently becoming "directionally challenged." To maneuver this stretch, they used the compass and the map. As they climbed the trail with their horses, the wind picked up, and dark, giant, egg-shaped clouds began blowing across the skies. In no time, they were stuck in the full throes of a blizzard. Maverick yelled out to the wagons, "Y'all, we need to find shelter fast! Take the wagons and horses over to the trees!"

The horses had winter coats and blankets, but no one really knew which, if any, had experienced a severe storm. It was complete mayhem!

Everyone and everything became drenched in a barrage of water falling from angry skies. The torrential downpour, with the clapping thunder and lightning storm, spooked the travelers and horses alike!

A tree was struck by lightning and split in two, with one half falling onto Maverick, pinning him to the ground. The wind blew with such a gale force that no one could hear his yells for help. Everyone was overtaken and blinded by the storm. The horses became flustered, bucking and whinnying as their eyes filled with fear. The pioneers tried to calm the horses and lead them to the shelter of the spruce forest nearby. Things went from bad to worse when the storm shortened out the Pigeon Phones. In the blink of an eye, everyone lost their grip and their way.

Eventually, the winds subsided, and Joseph thought that he heard a distant cry for help. He then realized that Maverick was nowhere to be seen. A dire foreboding instantly overtook him. He had to find him and fast!

The wagons, travelers, and horses were moved to better shelter, and Joseph circled back, searching for Maverick. He found him lying flat on his back, barely conscious under the fallen tree, moaning in pain. Seeing that Maverick could not move, an inner strength suddenly came over Joseph. He feared that if he didn't get him out from under that tree, Maverick would soon die. Joseph roused him and promised that he would save him, as Maverick cried out in terrible pain. Joseph then found a large branch and wedged it under the fallen trunk, pushing with all his might and finding a strength he'd never had before. The combination of Joseph's courage, determination, and adrenaline was what freed Maverick. As Joseph held the heavy tree up, Maverick used everything he had to move himself out from under the trunk. Once he was far enough away, Maverick lay in shock, semiconscious on the wet ground. Joseph removed his overcoat and covered him. They stayed there until the rain stopped, Joseph continuing to comfort Maverick and assure him that he would pull through. Eventually, the storm passed, leaving the earth saturated, the people disoriented, and the horses running amuck.

All night, Emma was beside herself with worry because both Joseph and Maverick had gone missing. At first, she was terrified and ran around in a panic, looking everywhere for them, to no avail. She soon returned to the wagon and held Junior close through the night, both of them crying, distraught and filled with fear. As the early morning sun rose, Joseph helped Maverick limp his way back to camp. Seeing them come over the mound, Emma and Junior ran to them, each doing their part to aid Maverick and get him to the warm fire.

Severely injured, Maverick was in excruciating pain, barely able to move. It was clear that he was too weak to lead the group. At this point, they hoped that Joseph had the wherewithal to take over. Maverick had seen a new side to Joseph and believed he could do it. The storm had put them in harm's way, and they could have all died. But Joseph stepped up. So did Emma. From the rescue, Maverick had a newfound respect and appreciation for them both. They had worked together to get through this calamity. Maverick now needed to rest, so Joseph and Emma took the reins to get them all through the pass. When the FOMOs gathered the horses and took a horse headcount, they realized that a few of the BTC horses were missing, which was a sizable financial loss. They were at risk of losing even more horses to exposure, as several of the younger horses were shivering uncontrollably, their blankets still drenched from the rain.

Maverick reached deep to find any reserve of energy he had left, but he couldn't find much. He'd been in storms before, but not like this.

Emma regretted that she allowed her emotions to get the better of her, especially in front of Junior. More importantly, she was embarrassed by her reckless behavior in the saloon after their unexpected windfall at the auction house. She realized that Joseph needed her strength and determination more than ever. From that moment, she vowed to herself that she would work hand in hand with Joseph, as partners, equally bearing the responsibility to get them through the pass and into the Hard Wallet Ranch Territory.

Seeing that Maverick was in no shape to guide them, Joseph took charge. "Everyone. Listen up. Reboot the Pigeon Phones and let's keep moving!" Several pioneers who had also been stuck in the storm helped the FOMOs get Maverick onto the wagon. Emma had thought she knew her husband, but she had never seen him like this. He was strong and exuded a new kind of confidence. "Grab the horses the best you can. We need to get through this damned pass!"

With the trail washed out, they used their Pigeon Phones to find a different route. Until then, everyone believed that the storm had shortened out the phones. What had actually happened was that the most infamous outlaws of Misdirection Mountain, the Rug Puller Gang, had used the storm as a cover to reshuffle and install new coordinates on the phone maps, leading the FOMOs toward the wrong trail on Misdirection Mountain.

SIDE NOTE

A "rug pull" is a crypto scam in which defrauders lie to the public to attract funding and quickly run off with investors' digital tokens.[7]

After traveling a few miles, Junior noticed that the position of the sun was off. The directions on his pigeon phone were off-target and had led them in the wrong direction! He pulled out the paper map, checking the coordinates with the compass. Junior's Pigeon Phone told him that they were heading north, but his compass showed the opposite! They'd been heading due south for a few hours. All of the pigeon phones had been hacked!

He turned to Maverick in a panic. "Maverick, we're off track!" He showed him the map. The ordeal of getting out of the forest had completely turned them around. They were now just a stone's throw from the foothills of Misdirection Mountain. Maverick's sense of alarm kicked in, which gave him a small burst of energy. He knew all too well what being turned around meant. They were in Rug Puller territory and needed to backtrack quickly or more horses would soon be gone! They quickly turned tail and left the foothills, then counted horse heads again. Even more horses were missing. Had the Rug Pullers already struck?

Junior felt smaller than a flea on the butt of a donkey, but Maverick was no stranger to these hacking predators. He swiftly thwarted this band's thieving ways by "white hacking" their map hack (see the next note on

---

[7] Definitions generated or vetted by ChatGPT, 2023, OpenAI, https://chat.openai.com. Rewritten for style and content.

"white hat" hackers), restoring the original map using his Pigeon Phone. The Rug Pullers Gang attack was stopped, but not without losses. Thank goodness Emma still had some winnings remaining from the card tournament! Only the ETH horses were large enough to pull the wagon, so hopefully they wouldn't have any more problems as they fought their way through Misdirection Mountain Pass.

Sadly, bad went to worse. Junior had lost track of Gumdrop who was far too delicate a breed for the demands of the trail and had been severely weakened from the storm. Having nothing left to give, Gumdrop simply laid himself down on the trail. When Junior finally found him, he could hear Gumdrop's very labored breathing. "It's going to be OK, little buddy; you'll be OK," Junior said, feeling like a dagger had just been stabbed into his sweet, young heart. Junior cried out as Gumdrop took his last breath. "Noooooooo!" Deep grief washed over him. It took the others a moment to understand what had Junior so upset. His unicorn, still on the ground, was now belly-up and gone. Junior stayed next to Gumdrop, stroking his colorful mane, willing with all his might that Gumdrop might come back to life. But Gumdrop had died. Junior sobbed. Not only had he lost his first real investment, but he'd also lost his animal friend! Junior's little unicorn pony would follow him, like a faithful puppy, their bond growing deeper each day. Gently, Emma finally led Junior away from deceased Gumdrop.

Maverick was sad for Junior and too weak to reprimand him for choosing a delicate breed. Those ponies don't fare well on a long, hard trail. Joseph tried to reassure Junior, but his timing was terrible. "Don't worry, Junior, we'll get you a new pony when we get to our new ranch."

"But it won't be Gumdrop!" said Junior, sobbing even harder now, shoulders shaking.

"Junior, I know it's hard, but we just can't let our emotions take over when it comes to buying horses," Emma said. "Anything can happen." Seeing Gumdrop's lifeless body, a memory flashed over Maverick, and he turned to Junior. "When I was a youngin'," he said weakly, "I had a unicorn pony too—it was attacked by a bear and died. I learned from that experience, and it made me better at selecting stronger horses. There are so many breeds to choose from. Knowing which horses are good for building out a strong herd takes time to learn. And, if you're lucky, you'll find a horse that will survive long enough to become a lifelong friend and make you a profit too."

"Don't get down on yourself," Maverick told Junior as they redirected their route. "If you hadn't noticed that we were off track when you did, we would have been in a much bigger heap of trouble and lost the whole herd. Junior, chin up."

Dear Reader,
While not so dramatic and physically painful as the FOMOs' experience, the crypto version of Misdirection Mountain is very real and nefarious. URL redirects by "black hat hackers" (bad guys) have taken many newbies by surprise. The "white hat hackers" (good guys) are hired to reverse the thievery and to audit system vulnerabilities as a form of due diligence. Again, stay modest when it comes to your successes. You can lose just as fast as you win.

A series of miracles got the FOMOs the rest of the way without incident, and the pioneers finally made it through the final leg of the pass. The first to arrive got the fires burning and set up a camp that was large enough for several families. After what they had all endured, no one could do enough to tend to and care for one another. The men helped Maverick out of the wagon with strong, gentle hands, placing him on a makeshift chair at the warm campfire. After a while, with all they had just been through, Junior asked Maverick why he risked everything to get a ranch in the Hard Wallet Ranch Territory. Having the Soft Wallet ranch seemed so much easier.

Maverick was quiet for a while, as if he might not answer the boy, but then he began in a sad voice, "I've had that Soft Wallet ranch for a while. There was an unfortunate occurrence that cost me all my animals, my crops, and my sweetheart."

Emma's interest was immediately spiked. "Really? How?"

"It started with another bad storm. The crops flooded and the animals were up to their ankles in water. With all of the chaos, Rug Pullers somehow snuck in and took everything they could grab, including all of the oxen, our bulls, horses, Tether ponies, sheep, and cows. A bad roof leak distracted us in the main house. Water was everywhere! We didn't realize that we were being robbed! When we understood what had happened, I was madder than a sack of hornets! I rounded up neighbors and we went tracking the bandits, all the way to Misdirection Mountain. We knew those thieves were there, but the mountain has a hidden cave system that only they could get in and out of. After hours of looking, that blasted band of misfit Rug Pullers was still nowhere to be found. They had my livestock inside that mountain and there was nothing any of us could do.

My sweet Sophia, that was her name, was all torn up. She left me before I got back, returning to her family. The mail carrier, Stagecoach Mary, saw how distraught she was and took her away. Most of what we owned in the house was ruined by the flood. All that Sophia left behind was a letter."

Maverick's face showed his deep sadness, and Emma's heart hurt just watching him. "Oh my . . . ," she said, "what did the letter say?" The letter remained in his inside jacket pocket tucked away, next to his heart. But he didn't need to pull it out to recount the words. "Dear Maverick, I'm sorry but life on the frontier for us has only been filled with sorrow, more than I can bear. I love you but I must leave. Stagecoach Mary has taken me back home. I'll be living with my sister. Please don't come for me. I'll never return."

Although he had held his cards close when it came to showing his love for her, Maverick cherished her with all his heart. He hated that he had failed her. Even though so much of what happened on the ranch was beyond anyone's control, his heart weighed heavy still, and for years, he had deeply grieved her leaving. But after she left, he moved on too, seeking a fresh start in the Hard Wallet Ranch Territory. Maverick's hard exterior had a crack, albeit small. His sadness made the FOMOs appreciate him even more. What he had endured seemed to have made him a stronger and an even more impassioned protector. No more words were exchanged. They tended to Maverick so he would be warm for the night by the fire, and then they somberly headed to their bedrolls. That blizzard, Maverick's sad tale, and the Rug Puller incident had shaken them.

Dear Reader,

It also happened to me...

We all face storms in life—you know, those huge disruptive tsunamis that leave us with only one option—to pivot and carry on in a different direction. My personal "storm of storms" happened when my father died shortly after being diagnosed with end-stage heart and lung disease in April 2010. Three years later, my mother, who also was in poor health, died in March 2013. Shortly before my mother's passing, my late husband was diagnosed with brain cancer. In September 2014, the cancer outsmarted the medicine, taking his life. The back-to-back losses of my loved ones put a gaping hole in my heart and set me adrift for a while. I was no longer a daughter, a wife, a caregiver, a stepmother, a dog owner, etc. Our home had been sold right before my husband died, so I had no physical or emotional home base. My daughter was attending university out of state, so my doting days were done... except for doting on myself, which I had never really done before.

Fortunately, I was buoyed by the love and support of my friends and family in my grief. This cluster of losses thrust me into the unknown, compelling me to find a new purpose. I promised myself that grief would not drive my life. It eventually lifted, and with time, I healed and found joy.

The FOMOs took to the frontier to find their new future. As much as they grieved their old life, the frontier gave them many gifts. They stayed united, they developed inner strength and new capacities, they found fellowship with others, and became clear on what mattered most for their family. Remember, dear reader, inside the pain and tough times in life, there are pearls of wisdom that allow us to turn our misfortunes into precious gems of all kinds.

STEP SEVEN: Safe at home

Prep Stage: Freddie's Plan
Stage One: Get Ready: Mindset, Money, and Mapping.
Stage Two: Shopping for Assets
Stage Three: Perils of the Journey
Stage Four: Get The Soft Wallet Ranch
Stage Five: Time to Trade
Stage Six: Don't Get Misdirected!
Stage Seven: Safe at Home

Traversing both the Soft Wallet Ranch Territory and the Misdirection Mountain Pass were the toughest parts of the journey. Even the horses were dragging. Hopefully, the difficulty would let up!

The last leg of the trail had them officially entering the Hard Wallet Ranch Territory. Something was different about these parts. Their deep fatigue was slowly replaced by wonder. The region had mountain peaks and beautiful valleys with winding rivers. With the trail's end, they were entering more remote terrain. Maverick assured them that the Hard Wallet ranches were less than a day's ride away as the crow flies. Still too injured to ride horseback, he had switched positions with Joseph. Joseph was now riding Maverick's horse, and Maverick had taken over the reins of the wagon, with Junior and Emma seated on each side of him. The trek to Freddie's ranch took most of the day. Once they arrived, what they saw took their breath away. Her ranch, affectionately called the F&S Ranch (for Freddie and Shane) commenced with a long, thin road. The vista beyond the ranch had them mesmerized by the snow-covered mountaintops, animals roaming, and the sprawling land beyond. Maverick's ranch neighbored Freddie's. In the final hour of their travel, he got a second wind thinking about the ranch Freddie had just recently built out. Unbeknownst to her cousins, Freddie had also secured and built out other ranches close to her to sell to pioneers and newbie ranchers coming to settle in this region. There was one in particular, adjacent to her ranch, that she had already made move-in-ready for her cousins, with a barn, a corral, and a main house. She had also installed a grand wraparound porch, perfect for star gazing. This magnificent ranch was a worthy fit for her family!

When Freddie saw them coming, she and Shane rode out to greet them. She couldn't disguise her worry when she saw that Maverick was in a bad way. The idea of anything happening to him was just too much! After Sophia left him, he guided Freddie to set up ranches. They became ranch partners and trusted friends. Freddie and her son both deeply admired that man, and she would take down anyone who dared hurt him! That was just her way.

"Maverick, what did you do to yourself? Damn you!" Maverick tried to deflect. "I'm fine, Freddie. Just a scratch."

"You flannel-mouthed liar!" she yelled. "You might have broken your leg! I'm sending a hand to get the doc." Freddie was fit to be tied, but Maverick knew she was relieved as she kept yelling at him. "You were supposed to get them here safe and sound, not get yourself all busted up!" With a high-handed attitude, she dramatically threw her hair back, turned around, and stormed away from him. The truth was, she was happy he only hurt his leg, and she did her best to hold back her tears. She then hollered louder than was required, "Let's get those wagons and horses inside!" The FOMOs rode into her ranch, taking in the massive corral, the two-story barn, and the main house tucked into the mountainside.

Shane held the main door to the house open as everyone did their part to help Maverick to the couch. Supper was in preparation by the cook while Freddie took them to the guest rooms so they could wash up and get some shut-eye before eating.

Later that afternoon the doctor made a visit to examine Maverick's injuries, wrapping his leg, giving him a potion for pain and instructing him to lay low for a while so he could heal. Freddie thanked the doctor, bidding him farewell before she called everyone to supper. "Cousins, I'm so proud of you! You made it. And I looked at those horses of yours. Well done! Fine horses you got! No crowbaits or bangtails." She smiled, nodding her approval.

Practically stuffing down their food, Joseph, Emma, and Junior finally came up for air and told Freddie and Shane about the blizzard, the Rug Puller Gang attacks, and the tree that fell on Maverick after the lightning struck. They recounted the stories about the pioneers they had befriended and traded with on the trail. Freddie listened intently as they described every detail. Much of it was painful to hear. Freddie wanted to change the mood.

Once the delicious red cream pie was served, she announced that she had a surprise for them.

"What, Freddie? Tell us."

"I found you a ranch and it has everything, including a covered porch with a swing. Truth to tell, I didn't just find it. I have the deed to it and built it, adding that porch. I know how much you love a swing, Joseph. The deed will be yours and the price will be just right." She winked at her cousins. "Do you want to go see it?"

Joseph and Emma went speechless for just a moment. Joseph looked at Freddie, holding back his emotions, but Emma grabbed Freddie and gave her a giant hug. They couldn't believe it. Joseph finally spoke. "Yes, Freddie. We'd love to. Thank you. Thank you." Then Emma grabbed the lot of them, hugging them all again, as a family. Freddie's family had finally arrived, and the FOMOs were safe. The shock started to wear off, and they all shed a few tears.

With Maverick now being ported around in a makeshift chair and put into the back of the wagon, Freddie and Shane took the family to their new home, christened the FOMO Family Ranch. It was pristine! The FOMOs felt the safe embrace of the mountains around them and had a sense of freedom they had never known. They fell in love with the porch and the swing and sat down to take in the view. It was the perfect platform for absorbing the expansive countryside and for simply watching the grass swaying to the afternoon breeze as the birds chased one another, chirping with joy. The FOMOs could sense their dream of becoming accomplished ranchers right at their fingertips.

Freddie had outdone herself. The main house was all arranged—cooking pans, beds, and all. And the corral was horse-ready, with the best lock around! In fact, Freddie had already had her ranch hands lead their horses to the new corral. Because of Maverick's special engineering skills, the

ranch was digitized and completely outfitted with automated hay-feeding stations and self-generating watering troughs.

They carried Maverick to the porch. Freddie stood next to him with her hand on his shoulder and spoke to them all. "Y'all, this is your ranch now. Here's the code for the barn door, your public and private keys for trading and receiving horses, and the seed phrase you'll need to open the lock of your corral. Maverick helped me install the latest technology for ranching a while back. This ranch is as special as you are. My ranch manager will help you get the hands you need for training and breeding, but you'll need less help with how we fixed up your horse feeding operation."

As Joseph took in the moment, his Ma and Pa came to mind. He wished they were all together here on this beautiful land. After all, if not for their sugar bowl money, his family might not have gotten here at all. Joseph closed his eyes, silently thanking Ma and Pa for their part in giving them a new start, even though it was a future they could never have imagined. Maverick interrupted his thoughts by calling for everyone's attention.

"Freddie, your cousins are ranchers now. I saw how they fought like banshees to survive the hardest storm I've ever seen. It was a bear! We could have all been done for and lost all of the horses, but Joseph found me and saved my hide as well as the horses. Joseph, Emma, and Junior really came together. They led all the travelers through the pass and now here we all are on this beautiful porch. Your cousins are ace-high amazing! Strong as bulls!

EPILOGUE

Come springtime, Joseph, Emma, and Junior headed back to the second auction house to trade. By this time, the FOMOs had a few younger ETH horses to sell and were now in the market for more breeding mares. They also wanted more BTC horses. A new herd of BTC horses was arriving at auction, and the starting bid prices were favorable because of the market swing. While Freddie and Maverick helped the FOMOs set up a very successful BTC horse breeding operation, the family had become true ranchers, now able to handle their own herd. Under Maverick's watch, Junior had become quite the horse trainer too. He transformed them from new bucking broncos into racers fast enough to bring home big purses in loads of regional horse races. As for navigating the terrain, Joseph took Junior and Shane hunting, shooting, and tracking every Saturday until the two boys could wander on their own. The region was known for bears that attacked horses, so they became agile at bear trapping to protect their livestock. The next generation was learning how to step into its own!

Before Joseph and Emma set out, Freddie brought over a hot pot of coffee. Joseph thought that Freddie would be joining them. "No, Joseph.

Y'all got this. I'm staying behind to secure more ranches. I want to help y'all expand your assets and find some ranch land we can build together for the new pioneers. I already told the auction house that you'd be buying for me in my stead. Emma, you've got the instincts for bidding. You do the horse-trading. I know you'll handle the buying and selling just fine. Just follow the strategy we talked about. And remember, stay modest. You'll never have the whole ranching business entirely figured out. You outdid yourselves at the auction before but continue to build your skills at acquiring good horses. Remember you can lose it all anytime. It's about staying focused, vigilant, and ahead of potential danger."

"Freddie, I still can't believe we've come this far," said Joseph. "We still have more to learn, but win or lose, we are grateful we are here with you, Shane, and Maverick. Nothing can break you when you have your family and friends standing with you."

Freddie's cousins looked out at the valley and the advent of the new day, feeling hopeful and prepared for what was to come. They had weathered the flood, the storm, grief, predators, bandits, and the rough terrain. There would always be risks, but they knew it was their destiny to carry on.

THE END

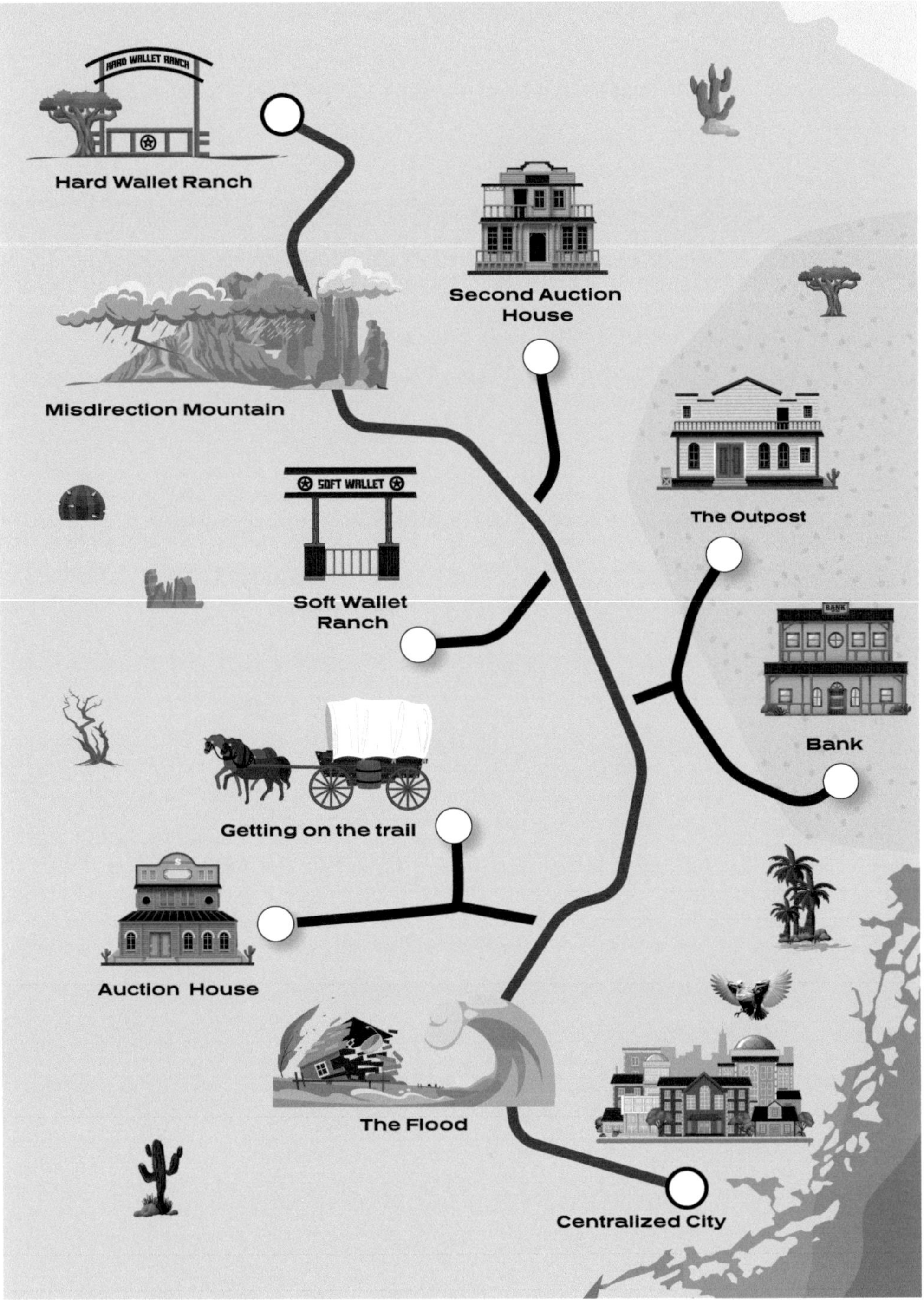

THE BLOCKCHAIN TRAIL

PART TWO
Your Journey

When it comes to the Wild West of crypto, a few friends of mine took every extra dollar they had and bought Bitcoin. Why would any sane person do that? I had to find out..

— MARYL GLADSTONE, AUTHOR

PREP STAGE: Your Game Plan

Crypto newbies, welcome to your new frontier!

You're about to saddle up and venture into the vast new landscape of digital asset investments. This digital Wild West is your untamed terrain teeming with both opportunities and challenges.

One of the first rules to understanding crypto is that taming crypto is not the point. The more worthwhile pursuit is to tame your inner frontier. Have you homed in on what drives you when it comes to investing? Is it FOMO that motivates you or is it forward-thinking? If you're not sure, I've created a quick survey that will give you some insight. Take it for a quick glimpse into your mindset around investing. Since our topic is cryptocurrencies as digital assets, the Investor Quiz is a useful starting point to help you with mapping out your quest (and your initial approach!). You might discover that you are the daring prospector type that prefers to hunt for gold and pan for riches in high-risk rivers, or you might instead be more of the steadfast homestead type, inclined to tilling the soil and planting steady gains over time. Some of you might already be savvy traders in a different asset class with skills that will transfer to this new frontier. By understanding your investment personality, the Investor Survey equips you with the insights to forge a path that aligns with your goals, works with your risk tolerance, and pays tribute to your adventurous or more cautious spirit. Knowing what kind of investment pioneer you are can be the difference between having a plan that gets you gold or has you losing your way in the crypto wilderness.

As you take to the trail, the equipment you'll need will depend on your skill level and how much of a newbie or veteran investor you are with digital assets. So, put on your cowboy hat, grab your survey map, and let's blaze a trail through the investment frontier with wisdom and self-awareness as you figure out where you will be soon staking your claim.

What Investor type are you?

You'll be navigating through seven stages to becoming a savvy digital investor. Before riding onto the trailhead, your map needs to include a few crucial coordinates. For example, it's important to define your end goal. Why invest in crypto and other digital assets? As for strategy, that will progress as you do. Most of you new to crypto start as gamblers then move into being speculators, then investors, then wealth builders, and then wealth keepers. Each of us has a different starting point in our investor journey.

Developing competencies around investing is a process. Wherever you start, as you practice and take small actions, you'll grow and develop skills.

The FOMOs learned that first and foremost, they would need to tame their emotions to manage the ups and downs of the frontier. They persevered because they understood their end goals. When Emma played cards, she showed her stripes as a tried-and-true gambler. She could do that well because, when it came to cards, she knew how to control her emotions, set limits and not be emotionally attached to keep playing should she lose her initial ten-dollar investment. If or when you acquire crypto or any investment that comes next, you'll also need to guard against getting emotionally tied to whatever you're trading for. Better to begin with the notion to have a bit of fun. In the story, you'll remember how attached Junior became to Gumdrop, his unicorn pony. Anyone new to digital assets can experience that same feeling of angst when the tides of prices turn which, if you allow it, can hinder you from getting back on your horse and moving forward in improving your skills of the game.

For our purpose of delving into this new investment frontier, there are five investor types.

- **The Gambler** Attracted to inexpensive and unproven investments, swayed to invest by the euphoria, sexy marketing, FOMO, and the exuberance of markets quickly rising. Emotions driven and prone to invest during extreme market upticks.

- **The Speculator** Adopts a strategic trading approach, buys assets during bear markets, invests in risky "cowboy" ventures often being the first-money-in investors, prone to spend beyond incoming cash flow.

- **The Investor** Adheres to long-term strategies, follows a buy-and-sell strategy, invests in high-quality, durable assets, is not swayed by emotions, prefers future-oriented assets, saves more than spends.

- **The Wealth Builder** Seeks out expert advice and management, focuses on leveraging assets to generate more wealth, actively invests, maintains ready liquidity for seizing lucrative investment opportunities, prioritizes wealth accumulation, and spends less than incoming cash flow by design.

- **Wealth Keeper**: Free to live on their terms, prioritize wealth preservation over accumulation, concentrates on legacy and empowering future generations. No longer confined by the need to closely manage cash flow.

No matter your natural investor type, you will be assuming different mindsets as you evolve in making your investment decisions and develop your skills as a savvy digital investor.

Follow this **TamingCryptoBook.com/Investor-type to take the investor quiz.

Before You invest: The Bulls and the Bears Can Both Be Your Friends.

I'm sure many of you are familiar with bull runs and bear runs. Here's a quick note about them, to familiarize you about market movement.

Markets don't plateau, they rise and fall. In a bull market, stock and crypto prices trend up while in a bear market, they trend down. These shifts in market dynamics can make for profitable opportunities for traders when they have the knowledge on how to use them.

You might remember the bear market of 2008 and the recession that came with it. Investors who were not strategically well-situated suffered major losses. Because markets are complex systems, bull and bear runs are difficult to predict with any precision. And, these complexities and the various economic drivers make it impossible to pinpoint a specific event that pivots markets. Like horses, markets are skittish and can respond erratically to news about geopolitical events, governmental policy changes, corporate earnings announcements, inflation predictions, etc. Anything that has a macro impact (real or imagined) can trigger bear or bull runs.

Some people believe they can time the market. Maybe if you are a more advanced day trader, there are ways to do that. Any expert will acknowledge that timing the market, really, is impossible. For crypto newbies, slowly acquiring a coin that you find worthy of the risk over time by dollar-cost averaging, then employing a profit-taking strategy, will help you ride the runs. I personally like to buy BTC and then hold it since it's considered the gold standard of crypto and has shown decent resilience to bear and bull runs.

Things to Ponder: Now We Get to WHY

Why Be a Digital Asset/Crypto Investor?

Maverick asked the FOMOs about what they imagined and envisioned for the future after they had bid on horses for the first time. Since every outcome is born from the imagination, thought and vision, I ask you to explore the same idea for yourself.

Tell me...
- What is driving you to step into crypto now or later (or ever)?

- What are your financial interests and goals? Do you have a long-term plan for your investments?
- For strategies, are you the buy-and-sell type, like a day trader, or do you prefer to buy and hold?
- Do you have a sense of your tolerance to risk?
- Do you know what digital assets are interesting to you?
- How much mad money will you begin with?

A starting plan will serve you now and as you go. Knowing your tendencies, intentions, and desires will help you avoid typical newbie pitfalls.

Like Roy Rogers loved to say, "You haven't missed the wagon train," especially now, with our economic systems and economies shifting at breakneck speed. Many new investment opportunities are emerging as blockchain evolves how business everywhere is being done.

Are You Ready for the New Digital Frontier?

It's your turn to start your journey, now, so grab your saddlebags, and let's get on the trail! Here are the seven stages to taming crypto as a digital asset investor:

>**Stage One**: Get Ready: Mindset, Money, and Mapping
>**Stage Two**: Shopping for Assets
>**Stage Three**: Perils of the Journey
>**Stage Four**: Get Your Soft Wallet

Stage Five: Time to Trade
Stage Six: Don't Get Misdirected!
Stage Seven: Safe at Home

Dear reader, carry this checklist with you as you start your journey with crypto.

Stages 1 and 2:

Stage 1:	Set aside some mad money.
Stage 1:	Find your guide and guidance.
Stage 2:	Use a reputable exchange in your country and apply the recommended security settings.
Stage 2:	Get comfortable navigating the exchange.
Stage 2:	Learn about the cryptocurrency you are interested in.

Stage 3: Security Checklist

Stage 3:	Use a strong password with a respected password manager app that also has a strong password. Maintain a list of your passwords offline.
Stage 3:	Use two-factor identification on only one device.

Stage 3:	Select the crypto wallets that will work with your crypto of choice (soft and hard wallets).
Stage 3:	Keep your devices updated with the latest software updates and use antivirus software.
Stage 3:	Use browsers and search engines that respect your data privacy.
Stage 3:	Manage your cookies on your browsers of choice..
Stage 3:	Set up a new encrypted email with an email provider that has stellar encryption systems..
Stage 3:	Don't be tempted to click on or follow suspicious emails and sources of any kind.
Stage 3:	Only disclose your digital asset activity to people that you trust.
Stage 3:	Select someone you trust with financial savvy to have access to your passwords if needed.
Stage 3:	**Optional: Use a VPN to mask your IP address as needed.

Stage 4: Soft Wallet

Stage 4:	Download and set up a soft wallet and order a hard wallet.
Stage 4:	Review the soft wallet strategy.

Stage 5: Trading

Stage 5:	Make your first trade.
Stage 5:	Transfer digital assets to your soft wallet of choice.

Stage 6: Don't Get Misdirected

Stage 6:	Input information and check the ledger.

Step 7: Safe at Home

Stage 7:	Set up your preferred hard wallet that you ordered directly from the hard wallet company.
Stage 7:	Understand what your seed phrase does.
Stage 7:	Safely store the seed phrases.
Stage 7:	Transfer digital assets to your hard wallet..
Stage 7:	Keep your own counsel when it comes to your digital asset holdings.
Stage 7:	Choose where you will store your actual hard wallet device.
Stage 7:	Make sure to give someone you trust a way to access your crypto hard wallet if you become incapacitated or die. Who can you count on that knows how to access digital wallets?

STAGE ONE: Get Ready: Mindset, Money, and Mapping

The terrain of crypto and blockchain is constantly changing, making it both interesting and stressful. Finding your way to profits is not for the faint of heart. The resilience that the FOMOs mobilized allowed them to stay focused even through their toughest moments as they forged ahead in pursuit of one main goal: to secure a Hard Wallet ranch and fill it with BTC horses. You, dear reader, will want to do that too. Having resilience and a plan will keep you composed and empowered to take only those actions that will benefit you.

So, what does that actually entail? No, not a long night of whiskey shots in the saloon, LOL!

- **FIRST:** Set aside mad money to begin with crypto.
- **SECOND:** Seek out help and information to support you in building your muscle for following a strategy for securing your new digital assets. Finding your very own Maverick wouldn't be a bad idea.
- **THIRD:** Have a plan for managing those digital assets and keeping them "secure" in wallets.
- **FOURTH:** Celebrate the victories along the way. They're always happening.

Freddie helped her cousins create a plan and roadmap that they fondly referred to as "Freddie's Way" to step into their new frontier. This helped them approach the frontier one stage at a time and gave them clarity on their next steps.

My advice? Please don't trip yourself up by critically judging any missteps that could happen as you progress. As much as there are external threats that are real to deal with, the bigger threat can come from inside your head. Stay focused on what you're here to learn, and stay off the emotional rollercoaster that market volatility can bring.

MINDSET: Venturing Into This New Frontier Takes Moxie and Courage!

In the story, the FOMOs faced a dilemma—to stay and endure the aftermath of the storm in Centralized City or venture into a whole new frontier. Their choice was less about itself and more about the mindset they would need to embrace and act from. How does this relate to you?

- Are you open to adopting new technologies?
- Can you discipline your emotions?
- Will you accept help to learn about digital asset literacy?
- Are you open to using security measures for your identity and your digital assets?
- Is it important to you to advance your thinking and optimize your life as our world changes?

MONEY: Mad Money: What Is It and How Can We Calculate It?

If you are completely new to crypto, I suggest that you start with a small amount of "mad money." That's what Joseph FOMO found in Ma and Pa's sugar bowl. Emma increased their stash of mad money with her purse winnings playing cards.

I am not much of a poker player myself, but I do go to Vegas on occasion. My mad money is what I'll spend when I travel to Vegas, all in, plus my monthly budget for hot chai lattes. Between Vegas and lattes, I came up with a mad money figure that I used to start with blockchain and cryptocurrencies. These funds were not "critical to pay my bills" money. They come from the "extras" bucket. Each of us has our own mad money number. Like Freddie did with her cousins, when you take a deep-dive look at your personal budget, your mad money allotment should be clear. Joseph found the courage to take to the trail when he discovered Ma and Pa's hidden sugar bowl funds. It's psychologically powerful to determine ahead of time a specific amount of mad money because it takes away the guilt associated with "wasting" and being careless with our personal funds. Mad money gives us breathing room to become better players of the crypto game and learn with less pressure. With mad money, we can experiment and learn new skills to move our financial goals forward without the knee jerk tendency to punish ourselves for unavoidable missteps.

In the FOMO story, their expenditures exceeded their mad money allotment. That was written for the sake of drama, but what they did is not any kind of drama you need. In fact, don't do what they did. As for the FOMOs' specific circumstance? All the FOMOs were excellent savers. Even Ma and Pa FOMO had a rainy-day fund with their sugar bowl money, pun intended. Because they saved and so did Ma and Pa, they were able to pivot after the flood disaster. Their foresight gave them options most people never have.

Just like horses, cryptocurrency has its own degree of risk. **Take the time to research a coin's purpose or utility, its market performance over time, its age and stage, and the developers and engineers that are behind it.** If you recall, Johnny B., a pioneer and newbie rancher, had no choice but to sell his best ETH horses because he did not get guidance or employ a guide like Maverick to help him with his initial horse buying for his soft wallet ranch. If, after my filtering process, a coin holds an interesting profit potential, I will allocate mad money for it. Reducing risk is not an exact science, but using the latest market data helps with return yields more than betting on some random coin you know nothing about. Once I vet a crypto coin for my holdings, I start with a small position.

What's Up with Those Gas Fees?

A dollar can go far when it comes to cryptocurrencies as compared to stocks because crypto exchanges generally have low trading minimums, even $5 or $10. But gas fees vary based on how active the networks are at different times of the day. At peak trading times, gas fees can cost as much as the crypto with super-small transaction amounts and the fees can exceed the cost of the coin. Figure out ahead of time how much mad money you'd like to spend for a cryptocurrency coin or another digital asset, and see if the transaction makes financial sense. That's what Emma did when she bid at the second auction house. She waited to bid until the second round when the horse prices fell, and so did the fees. Don't get taken by surprise by the fees! There will be surprises along the way, but the gas fees don't have to be one of them.

Mapping the Landscape

Before the FOMOs stepped foot into the auction house, Freddie had already reviewed the order of things with them, including what they would be doing and where they would be going. Your map will do the same thing. You'll see where you'll be prepping, where you'll be shopping, where you'll be stopping, and where you'll be trading. In this process there will be risks to defend against and assess. Take the time to learn how to set yourself up well when it comes to finding opportunities that match your stage and your goals as you enter your digital asset journey. There's much to gain as you develop your acumen.

Considering how big of an asset class crypto now is, it's hard to discern, as a digital asset investor, whether it is riskier to act now in securing crypto digital assets, or if the greater risk is waiting or "falling behind" as the appeal and demand for crypto increases and more cryptocurrencies come to market. This decision is personal, and we have a window that's currently open for acquiring decentralized cryptocurrencies like ETH and BTC. There are no economic crystal balls, but since the days of Caesar, governments and central banks have controlled the money supply for society. Digital coins created by the U.S. government called Centralized Digital Bank Currencies (CBDCs) are set to be introduced into the United States in 2023/2024. When CBDC is fully implemented, the roles that DeFi cryptocurrencies like BTC and ETH will play will hopefully become more defined around the world. On the global stage, there are a few countries that have adopted BTC and other cryptocurrencies as additional forms of money, incorporating them into their economies, such as El Salvador. On the other side of the spectrum, a google search shows several countries that have banned DeFi cryptocurrencies, such as Algeria, Egypt, and

China, to name a few. So, while the window to invest in cryptocurrencies is open, if it suits your plan, then join the "economic revolution" in whatever way makes sense. To make traveling easier, many globetrotters like having access to cryptocurrency as an alternative source of funds when they hop from country to country. There are Bitcoin ATMs around the world now as we speak.

Investing in blockchain technologies is for early pioneers who have the mad money and appetite for some risk and potentially exciting rewards. Like the Wild West, it's got its own lure. If you are called to be a part of the digital frontier, the reality is that few succeed, especially if they aren't properly equipped.

Dear Reader, to Reiterate, to Repeat, as a Strong Reminder, in Full Disclosure...

- **This digital frontier is filled with uncertainty and volatility**: The charts tracking gains have shown astronomical returns, but prices fluctuate dramatically in short periods, and future values are impossible to predict.

- **Just like any other financial market, crypto has both bull and bear markets**: A bull market is a sustained stretch of time when investment prices are rising. When markets have a bull run, every stock, fund, or cryptocurrency will seem like a strong and viable investment. The true test is when a market has a bear run, which is a market that has a sustained stretch of declining prices. You'll get a sense of how strong your cryptocurrency or other asset is by how it responds when the bear market is done.

- **Digital asset investments are high-risk**: Investing in cryptocurrency is like prospecting and mining for gold during the gold rush days. There is at least as much potential for losses as there are for gains.

- **Right now, there's no FDIC insurance or traditional regulation to protect consumers:** While our banks are regulated and have the FDIC to back the funds we keep with banks, cryptocurrencies don't have those protections. Like the Wild West was, it's more like a "lawless" frontier.

- **Opportunities for innovation**: As with the start of the Wild West, innovation was disruptive and exponential! That's no different now. Workers laid down hundreds of miles of railroad tracks that opened nations up to expansive commerce; blockchain is providing new rails that underlie new technologies and business opportunities today globally.

STAGE TWO: Shopping for Assets

"We FOMOs don't venture into new frontiers unprepared, and neither will you." —**Freddie Fomo**

- **Select an exchange**
- **Get an account**
- **Pick your cryptocurrency coins**
- **Buy**

Like horses, getting your hands on crypto is easy to do once you pick your exchange.

We can head to the exchange now, but to which one? Freddie and Maverick had their preferred auction houses. The trusted auction houses that had the horse selections they wanted, had passed the test of time, and were good service providers.

How Do You Pick a Good Crypto Exchange?

1. Is it reputable, secure, and widely used?
2. Does the exchange have a good user experience, and does it offer customer support?
3. What kind of cryptocurrencies are available?

In fact, let's revisit Mavericks seven criteria for what you need to know about a crypto exchange.

Maverick's Seven Criteria for a Crypto Exchange

	Auction House	Crypto Exchange
Criteria 1	The auction house's longevity	How established and active is the exchange?
Criteria 2	Stellar horse inventory	What cryptocurrencies does the exchange platform feature? Do they have the more established cryptocurrencies??
Criteria 3	How secure and safe it is. Have they had bandit attacks? Did the auction house protect the ranchers' purchases?	Has the exchange ever been hacked? Are there complaints about the exchange? Search to find out.
Criteria 4	Is the auction house respected by the community?	Is it well-funded? Look at their trading volume and online portfolio. How is customer support?
Criteria 5	Do they work with more seasoned ranchers?	Does the exchange offer opportunities and lower fees for more seasoned traders?
Criteria 6	Can you take your horses right after you've placed your bids or is there a holding period?	Does the exchange have a transfer delay for your crypto? Do they have security holds on funds and trades?
Criteria 7	How do they surpass their competitors?	Are there specific benefits on that exchange?

Investopedia.com lists their top choices for cryptocurrency exchanges (as of March 31, 2023):

- Best for Low Fees: **Kraken**
- Best for Experienced Traders: **Kraken**
- Best for Beginners: **Coinbase**
- Best Mobile App: **Crypto.com**
- Best for Security: **Gemini**
- Best for Altcoins: **BitMart Exchange**
- Best for Bitcoin: **Cash App**
- Best Decentralized Exchange: **Bisq**

Dear Reader,
Just as the FOMOs did when they first did business at the auction house, you'll also set up an account with the cryptocurrency exchange.

- The exchanges will verify your identity, just like a bank. This process is called KYC (know your customer), where you show your proof of citizenship or other identifying documents.
- You'll set up a method of payment. Since they won't take a chest of gold coins, you can link your existing bank account or use a debit card. Some exchanges accept PayPal, Venmo, and even Apple Pay. Each exchange will list payment methods they work with.

How to Buy Your First Cryptocurrency

Picking a coin:

1. Log onto to coinmarketcap.com. This is a trusted industry source for detailed information on coins and tokens.
2. As you begin, focus on coins that are listed in the top ten in terms of trading volume.
3. Markets are volatile, so as you start, hold off acquiring a coin if the markets seem extremely erratic. Raging bull or bear markets are never good times to enter any financial market.

My Journey as a Crypto Newbie

One thing I know is that anything I need I can find in my networks and communities. Once I realized that my investment advisors were not equipped to get me launched with digital assets, I reached out to a few of my financially savvy friends and asked them to refer me to good sources of information. I followed those leads and recommendations until I found a few different people that had been trading crypto for many years. As for scouring the internet, I knew that, for me, that would confuse more than help me, so that was not where I started.

The people I finally connected with were very generous in helping me select an exchange, pick my first few cryptocurrencies, and set up a crypto wallet. But I knew I wanted to actually learn more about how to evaluate and manage digital assets. One of the experts was offering short trainings for people new to crypto. So, I registered for the trainings and different classes and learned about security, privacy, wallets, hackers, transfers, exchanges, swapping sites, trading pairs, and more.

Before trading anything, what was hammered into us was that privacy and security come before anything else. We were advised to orient all we do with security and privacy ahead of any other priority. To that end, this is **WHAT I DID**.

- I was advised to **use the most secure browser** available that would be technologically compatible with the equipment I would be using for acquiring and trading crypto that would not capture my search data or IP address. My advisors recommended BRAVE and TOR. I used both but TOR was not as functional as BRAVE, so I primarily use BRAVE.

- I was advised to **use the search engine that was the least intrusive for gathering search data for marketing**. At the time, they recommended the search engine called DuckDuckGo. That's the one I use now. Each of us is responsible to check on the privacy settings on any browsers and search engines.

- I was advised to **set up a new, encrypted email** for transaction records and verification purposes. The provider of choice was Protonmail, that is the provider I use. I continue to use research email providers and create a new email address from time to time. It's wise to assume that any emails, addresses, passwords, and phone numbers that we've been using are possibly compromised by data harvesting.

- Coinbase is a good place as a beginning platform. I was advised to **put dollars into Coinbase and then buy the stablecoins known as**, USDT Tether and USDC. I opened up an account on Coinbase using a debit card for the source of payment. I then secured some stablecoin and waited until my cryptocurrency buys were no longer "on hold" on the exchange.

- For more **unique coins**, I was advised to open up an account on Kucoin. Kucoin is a next-level exchange, similar to the auction house that Freddie use to trade for specialized horse breeds. To use Kucoin, I transferred USDT from Coinbase since they don't work with fiat currency like dollars or any centralized money.

- I liked Coinbase because it was easy to use. What I didn't like was how many days I had to wait until I could transfer that crypto into a crypto wallet. The extended holding period was off putting.. I also didn't care for the higher gas fees Coinbase had compared to Kucoin when swapping. Coinbase now has a solution for the higher fees with their subscription model, like Amazon Prime or Audible. Instead of free shipping, it covers fees now, but it didn't when I started. Coinbase did have CoinbasePro, which helped with the gas fees, but the user experience was not ideal. The screen was hard to read.

DUE DILIGENCE TIP: Whenever trading, make a point to keep tabs on the fees because fee policies change frequently.

- I didn't like Kucoin because the user experience was not highly intuitive at the time. What I did like is that Kucoin had newer coins that Coinbase didn't. I also found myself challenged by the trading passwords Kucoin requires.

STAGE THREE: Perils of the Journey – Fortify Security.

Take Privacy and Security into Your Own Hands: A Deeper Dive on the Checklist

As for digital assets on the DeFi (decentralized finance) frontier, see yourself as a solo banker that does your own peer-to-peer (direct) transactions, with no official middleman to assist or protect you. That means that it's up to you and only you. Because of that, a good portion of this section sheds light on security actions that can help you set up more securely. Unlike Centralized City, which had a governing council, the frontier has no "sheriff" or centralized authority for protection. In banking and stock trading, we rely on institutions for asset protection. When it comes to DeFi, you need to keep your rifles loaded by having the best security settings available today.

Technology is calling us to see security differently. Because of that, follow the checklist of practical steps to guide you in getting started with cryptocurrency securely. If decentralized digital currencies are part of our future (and I believe they will be), then having good security routines is key. For your convenience, here it is again.

State 3:	Use a strong password with a respected password manager app that also has a strong password. Maintain a list of your passwords offline.
State 3:	Use two-factor identification on only one device.
State 3:	Select the crypto wallets that will work with your crypto of choice (soft and hard wallets).
State 3:	Keep your devices updated with the latest software updates and use antivirus software.
State 3:	Use browsers and search engines that respect your data privacy.
State 3:	Manage your cookies on your browsers of choice.
State 3:	Set up a new encrypted email with an email provider that has stellar encryption systems.
State 3:	Don't be tempted to click on or follow suspicious emails and sources of any kind.
State 3:	Only disclose your digital asset activity to people that you trust.
State 3:	Select someone you trust with financial savvy to have access to your passwords if needed.
State 3	**Optional: Use a VPN to mask your IP address as needed.

Since You're on Your Own, in These Early Stages Arm Yourself with Knowledge...

BROWSERS: Pick a Browser That Does Not Gather Your Data

Not all browsers and search engines are created equal!

Browsers are your gateway to the internet, so choosing a secure browser is an easy action you can take for privacy and security. Many browsers and search engines are data collectors. It's illuminating to understand which browsers are more geared toward respecting data privacy and which aren't. Many people browse the web with Google Chrome using the Google search engine, not knowing their data is being collected and repurposed. Search activity is not private.

I like the Brave Browser since it can minimize the risk of cookies and IP address exposure. A good browser needs to protect you from phishing sites, spyware, malicious ads/pop-ups, and web trackers. The software is changing constantly, so always activate browser updates, and every so often do a quick check on which browsers are highly rated for security.

Why not take a moment and do that right now?

Computer and Software Hygiene

he FOMOs scored the Soft Wallet ranch from the Smith Family because Mr. Smith had been remiss in keeping the lock on their corral updated. After losing all of their horses, they had no choice but to sell. In the real world, staying on top of updates is essential—for your wallets, for your browsers, for your computer, for your phones. It's a good rule of thumb to allow automatic updates so any glitches or fixes can be resolved before it causes problems for you.

Search Engines

For internet searches, I like the DuckDuckGo search engine. Its motto is "Privacy Simplified," and the company claims that it does not track and collect data, unlike Google, which tracks your searches with hidden trackers on millions of websites.

> *Combining the Brave browser with DuckDuckGo gives your personal information stronger protection against data tracking.*

Encrypted Email

It's a good practice to use secure email, especially when dealing with cryptocurrency transactions and any financially sensitive information. A company that was created expressly for encrypted email is Proton Mail (https://mail.proton.me). Based in Switzerland, Proton Mail is the largest encrypted email service in the world, used by journalists, activists, and businesses. I recommend using it to set up a new email because of its robust encryption features that make it virtually impossible for anyone to read email except the sender and the recipient.

Two-Step Verification

Using an authenticator app on your phone or computer for two-step verification is another move toward securing your accounts. An authenticator app digitally authenticates you as the person in possession of your devices and is another way to foil hackers looking for easy targets. When you enable two-step verification, an outsider will need not only your login credentials but also physical access to your phone or computer to hack your account.

The authenticator apps generate unique, time-sensitive codes that you use to enter during the login process. By requiring both your password and a code from the app, two-step verification makes sure that even if your password is compromised, your account stays secure. The authenticator apps I've used are Authy, Authenticator, and Twilio.

You may think that an authenticator app is unnecessary and that the SMS two-factor authentication (2FA) on your phone is enough. ROOKIE MISTAKE, newbie! Using SMS authentication for 2FA is risky, comparatively speaking. Hackers can use good old-fashioned spoofing, often combined with phishing, to intercept and read your SMS messages. SIM swapping is a common hacker ploy where hackers call your phone company, pretending to be a victim, and activate a new phone with your number, which gives them control of your phone number.

Ultimately, phones are designed for convenience, not security.

Oh, hackers and the tangled webs they weave! If they get ahold of your data, they can cause all kinds of headaches, including identity theft, stolen assets, and reputational harm. Without taking proper security measures, we should expect the unexpected.

You're Only as Good as Your (Pass)Word

When it comes to safeguarding, creating robust passwords is a good habit to have, and experts today say it is essential. To enhance security, choose complex passwords that are a long chain of numbers, letters, and symbols. A very long password that contains a diverse mix of characters is a deterrent for potential hackers. Hackers don't guess passwords. They have much more sophisticated ways to break in. Having longer and more complex passwords is an action we can take, and the stronger and longer, the better. While it's not an airtight solution, having a strong password is an important part of a comprehensive security strategy for safeguarding any assets.

Tips for Selecting Passwords[8]

- Never include personal information such as your name, your birthday, your username, or your email address, since all of this information is easily accessed in the public domain, and using those bits of data weakens your passwords.

- Use a password that is a minimum of twelve characters. According to Microsoft, fourteen is even better. The longer the password, the more armored you are against data breaches or cyberattacks.

- Each account needs its own password. I know, I know! What a pain with as many accounts as you have, right? Regardless, don't reuse

---

[8]*See resource section for more details on passwords.*
www.tamingcyptobook.com/resources

the same password for each account, especially not your financial accounts! If a hacker uncovers your password for one account, all of your other accounts could become compromised. the same password for each account, especially not your financial accounts! If a hacker uncovers your password for one account, all of your other accounts could become compromised.

- Refrain from using common phrases. Yes, they are easier to remember, but they are also easier to crack.

- Change your passwords according to what that account recommends. Recommendations from banks might differ from the recommendation of a crypto exchange. I tend to change passwords for financial and health accounts when I log in. I'll even select "forgot password" and modify it right then.

A Cybersecurity Expert's Password Management Hack

One of my cybersecurity pros uses LastPass, a password and data storage app that can be downloaded onto mobile phones and computers. Think of LastPass as a password vault where users store all kinds of data for every account they have. His secret sauce is having a master password for his LastPass vault that is over fifty characters long! Rather than changing each individual account's password that he stores on LastPass, he modifies the master password often so he's not an easy target for hacking. This expert did remind me that the LastPass master password needs to be memorized and/or stored offline, not on a mobile phone that's connected to the internet. According to NBC News[9], there is debate about how often to change passwords and how effective frequent password changes are in staving off cyberattacks. Each account needs to be reviewed on a case-by-case basis.

My favorite way to create a password is to take three words that don't go together, connect them, then insert numbers and symbols. An example is:

STapler-whiTE-sunRISE@4%4

Unfortunately, hackers use sophisticated programs that can break just about any password. Take on the habit of changing your password immediately when you get notices from companies about cyberattacks.

Don't Take Password Shortcuts—They Can Take You Down a Long, Hard Road

Storing data on your devices and in the cloud makes anyone more vulnerable to being hacked since devices that are online are the gateway. I learned certain methods to store passwords, private keys, and seed phrases that would keep them safely stored. As you set up your new emails and other accounts, have a special journal (a physical ledger or notebook) where you physically write down these things as they are created. This extra measure of security keeps your passwords offline. Your ledger can

---

[9] Melanie Pinola, "How often should you change your passwords?" NBC NEWs, www.nbcnews.com/technolog/how-often-should-you-change-your-passwords-1C7511554 Accessed March 2023.

store all your passwords and account and website login details in one place and keep your online web account information and user data safe.

A more modern approach to keeping your information safe and offline is to have a spreadsheet that is stored on an external thumb drive that you insert and use to copy and paste. The point is to keep your passwords and so forth off your computer, away from the cloud. In short, find a system for storing private keys, passwords, and seed phrases offline. Password-storing apps (like LastPass or Dashlane) can be used, but judiciously. Refer to the text box above about LastPass. When it comes to passwords and cybersecurity in general, shortcuts can create vulnerabilities. It's almost like leaving your house keys in the door!

For those who want to take crypto to the next level and incorporate digital assets into an investment process, you might consider securing separate equipment that would be used exclusively for investing, such as a dedicated laptop, cellphone, and hard drives, and so forth to perform the transactions in a more streamlined and secure way.

Name: _____
Site address: _____
Login/username: _____
Password: _____
Notes: _____
_____
_____

Keeping Track

Find your best solution for tracking and maintaining a clear and organized record of your cryptocurrency transactions. Doing that is important for tax purposes and to manage the performance of your digital assets. There are a few options I've tried. One approach is using a digital ledger, like a spreadsheet, to track your purchases and positions. Alternatively, there are user-friendly software apps, like TurboTax, Coinly, and CoinTracker, that can automatically manage this information for you as they connect to your exchange and extract the data on your behalf.

To create your own spreadsheet, there are sample templates online that you can customize according to your needs. CoinAtlas investment tracker is a free Google Spreadsheet template for both cryptocurrency and stock investors. Updating your records whenever you buy or sell cryptocurrencies is the easiest way that I've found to handle this administrative issue. To keep this information secure, you can store this transaction spreadsheet on the same USB thumb drive that you use for your passwords.

Who's Got Your Back? Decide Ahead of Time

Is there someone you trust to help you manage your affairs when that time comes? Better to figure that out well ahead of finding yourself needing their assistance. Whomever that person is, make sure they can gain access to your master password should you not be able to. Getting ahead of this before the unexpected hits will be much easier for fast support, especially when it comes to digital assets. If your trusted person doesn't know about crypto, then teach them how to access your digital assets.

Organize now to ensure that what you have is accessible for you and your heirs when that becomes important.

Clearing Memory Lane

Think of cache as a browser's short-term memory. When you visit a website, the browser stores a copy of the website's content (like pictures and text) on your computer so that if you visit that same website again, the browser can quickly retrieve the cached content instead of downloading it all over again, and that data can be served faster. If you are using a public or shared computer, clearing your cache may help protect your privacy. If you don't clear your cache, anyone who uses the computer after you may be able to see your browsing history.

Cookies, on the other hand, are like digital tags that websites put on your computer to remember things about you, such as your login information or preferences. For example, if you visit a shopping website and add items to your cart, the website will use cookies to remember what you added to your cart so that when you come back later, the website remembers what you wanted to buy. Cookies can also be used to remember your browsing history or to show you personalized ads based on your interests. Removing cookies can help you stave off the risk of privacy breaches. It can also reset your browser tracking and personalization.

Please don't underestimate the importance of clearing the cache and adjusting your browser settings to manage cookie tracking. Since cookies are embedded in almost everything, find a few quick tutorials about cookies to understand when and how to manage them. What to do and how to do it is not a cookie-cutter process, pardon the pun.

Cover Your Tracks with a VPN!
(Not Critical for Newbies, but Good to Know)

For an added security boost, crypto veterans often use a VPN, short for *virtual private network*. The FOMOs did something similar to bolster security when they circled the wagons one evening to avoid the black hat hacker bandits. VPNs encrypt your internet activity and route it through the VPN's server prior to connecting to a website, app, or any online service. VPNs can significantly boost online privacy by concealing and encrypting your IP address and location, which simultaneously encrypts your data and protects your identity.

You probably already know this but avoid using public WiFi to access APPS or financial accounts since these networks are vulnerable to cyberattacks, especially in places like train stations and airports. Better to use your cellphone's hotspot, your personal home WiFi, or any trusted connection. My cybersecurity pros respect TunnelBear and IPVanish as VPN options. Take a moment to research which VPNs are legitimate and the most reputable, then determine which level of VPN you'd like, as there are both free and paid options.

VPNs provide certain advantages for security, and they aren't perfect. The drawbacks differ for everyone but commonly have to do with location, connection, and other user-specific issues. Installing VPNs properly makes a difference. Not done well, they can interfere with certain programs and apps, which is really frustrating. Still, as VPN providers develop ways to simplify their user interface, it will enable everyone to use all the features they offer. *As with all things I recommend, do your due diligence before downloading a VPN.*

WHAT I DID

Each week, as beginner crypto traders, our guide would give us sequential directives on how to set ourselves up for early success. For her, success started with key security practices.

The first action she gave us was to create a special, unique space for doing focused work. I have a small office that I used to use exclusively for that. She recommended that the area be private and quiet with enough space to spread out. The purpose for this was to create consistent practices and not pollute the trades or compromise security with unwanted distractions. She encouraged us to put our game day hats on by mentally readying ourselves for swapping, starting with putting cellphones and computers on silence.

The second action for more serious crypto investors was having hardware and devices that were strictly for crypto. To that end, the more advanced students secured special hard drives or never used laptops, and even crypto-only cell phones. She warned the class to never mix business and pleasure when trading. When it came to the business of crypto, the world would need to be shut out, at least in the beginning. I made it a point to not check emails or log into any social media, because in the wrong environment, it was too easy to compromise the integrity of any transactions taking place.

The third action was to maintain all passwords, seed phrases, and sending and receiving addresses outside of the cloud. As beginners, she suggested we jot down our passwords, seed phrases, and other relevant numbers in an actual physical notebook that would always be kept in the special workspace.

The fourth action she gave to us was to set up two-step verification on our phones using Authy and Authenticator. She gave us this warning: only install the two-step verification apps on our phones, not on our computers. Hackers love it when they can hack your computer and initiate two-step verification without you realizing it. That can happen when you install the same authentication app on more than one device. The FOMOs went through something similar when they journeyed through Misdirection Mountain and the bandits commandeered their Pigeon Phones, re-routing their coordinates to the wrong trail, causing them to lose more horses.

The fifth action she gave us was to remember to always keep our software and hardware updated. When I've lapsed on that, glitches find me faster than a mosquito that hasn't eaten for a week!

Other actions that were recommended:

- **Follow the news.** I have a few subscriptions including a paid subscription to WIRED, and take advantage of the free resources from industry leaders like COINDESK.

- She emphasized to **NEVER autosave log-in information** on the browsers, as that puts the log-in information in the cloud.

- **Get a separate, new phone for account verifications** that is a pay-as-you-go phone so your personal contact information cannot be hacked.

- **Regularly clear browsing history** and clean out cookies. Boring, maybe, but it's good computer hygiene.

- Have a **spreadsheet habit**.

Dear Reader,
NOT YOUR KEYS, NOT YOUR CRYPTO
   Chase Danzig, who runs the Bitcoin Express YouTube channel, explains, "Crypto is always stored on the blockchain. It's not stored on some computer. It's not stored in the cloud. It's not even stored on a hardware wallet. It's always on the blockchain. What is stored on those devices is the keys that control the crypto and if you have your crypto on an exchange, then they, (a third party), have the keys to control the crypto. By keeping your crypto in a self-custody wallet, you have the keys to control your crypto."

   Bad actors aren't fiction. In our digital era, they hack, steal, disrupt, and undo security measures. The cryptojackers plagued the Wild West wherever they could! Security is done in layers. Using multiple layers of security for your computer, your transactions, and your assets helps you substantially reduce your vulnerability to potential threats. Wouldn't you rather relax a bit and ride the trail than be on constant alert, expecting to become some cryptojacker's next victim? This will free you up to focus more on trading and managing digital assets than stressing over those who would prey on you.

Here are a few ways crypto newbies can get blindsided:

- With "pump and dump" cryptocurrency schemes, the global white-collar crimes de jour
- By picking a poorly run exchange
- By using low-security browsers

My Journey: What I Did (Wrong)
Don't Try Any Fancy Footwork Until You've Mastered the Steps!

"Technical complexity is part of the risk mode... If your security is more technically complex than your level of skill, then you introduce a very serious risk that you will lose your crypto. Not because it is stolen, but because your ambition for technical excellence exceeded your skill level for technical execution and you frankly messed it up."
—ANDREAS M. ANTONOPOULOS, BRITISH-GREEK BITCOIN ADVOCATE, TECH ENTREPRENEUR, AND AUTHOR

True story: In preparing to buy an altcoin, I worked with my IT friend to transfer money from my hard wallet to my soft wallet. In the interest of safety, we attempted to insert an extra layer of security to protect the funds while they sat in the soft wallet. I've transferred digital assets before from the hard wallet to the soft wallet without a glitch. Not this time. By electing that extra layer of protection, I triggered an unusual technological anomaly.

When I typed in my password twice, I inadvertently entered one of the characters incorrectly the first time. In this transfer, there is no option to "see" what you are typing. When I received the error message that the passwords did not match, I pushed the backspace and that "locked in" the new, incorrectly typed password. I was then locked out of accessing those funds due to this glitch; I now had a new, incorrect password tied to the soft wallet.

Much to my chagrin, the mechanism changed my password to whatever it was that I had accidentally typed in! I did not push "save" or "OK." When I got the error message, I simply attempted to exit and type my password again, but I could not.

After going around and around with my IT friend and customer service, we found out that there was no fix. The only remedy is to attempt to recreate my typing error in order to release the funds from that wallet. I had to play around with all the possible variations of my password to see which accidental combination would gain me access. Otherwise, the funds will remain there forever. Ugh! Luckily, this is my chai latte money, so I'm not feeling terribly bad about it. This is your reminder—use your mad money. Glitches will find you too.

STAGE FOUR: Get Your Soft Wallet

Safety Versus Convenience

If you've decided to buy a bit of crypto, you'll want to transfer it onto a digital wallet.

Just like the FOMOs set up a soft wallet ranch to make it easier to horse trade, you'll want a soft wallet that stores your digital asset/crypto purchases, especially the stablecoins like UDST and USDC. Strong stablecoin in your soft wallet will have you ready to trade when a good buy opportunity presents itself.

Recall that, because of limited security, the FOMOs did not keep their best horses at their soft wallet ranch for very long, because it was not as secure as their hard wallet ranch. Their soft wallet ranch held their less valuable horses for quick horse trading and swapping while their hard wallet ranch would house their highly sought after BTC horses that they would buy and hold.

As a digital asset investor, you'll want both a soft and a hard wallet. These wallets essentially store the keys to your crypto and digital assets. They do not store the actual cryptocurrencies. Those are stored when they are officially recorded on the blockchain. The soft wallets are digital applications for storing and accessing your digital assets like cryptocurrencies and NFTs[10]. Soft wallets are often more susceptible to hackers because the keys are stored digitally; so, if your device is compromised,

---

[10] *An NFT is a digital asset that can come in the form of art, music, in-game items, videos, and more. They are bought and sold online, frequently with cryptocurrency, and they are generally encoded with the same underlying software as many cryptos. See resources page: tamingcryptobook.com/resources*

a hacker may gain access to your keys and might then be able to transfer your assets out of your digital wallet. Hard wallets, on the other hand, are much more secure because even if your computer is compromised, the keys are stored on the physical device, which are not automatically accessed via the internet. This makes the hard wallet more secure and a safer place to keep your most treasured digital assets, albeit the least convenient.

My Soft Wallet Strategy
Storing cryptocurrency on your soft wallet gives you quick and easy access. Many people keep their soft wallet apps on their phones for that reason. Just like the FOMOs did when they bid for the Tether ponies at the first auction house, leaving some on credit at the auction house and some for the trail, I like keeping some stablecoins in crypto as well as on my digital soft wallet so I can swap and trade anytime. Stablecoins are accepted by most exchanges for swapping or trading for other cryptocurrencies, like Bitcoin or Algorand. (Recall that the FOMOs kept their Tether ponies on their soft wallet ranch so they could trade them for more valuable horses like the BTC horses or the Algo horses.)

Which Soft Wallet, You Ask?
Money.com rated their top picks for the Best Crypto Soft Wallets as of March 2023. They are:

- **Coinbase Wallet**—Best for Beginners
- **MetaMask**—Best for Ethereum
- **TrustWallet**—Best for Mobile

- **Ledger Nano S Plus**—Best Hardware Crypto Wallet
- **Electrum**—Best Desktop Bitcoin Wallet
- **BlueWallet**—Best Mobile Bitcoin Wallet
- **Exodus**—Best for Desktop
- **Crypto.com**—Best DeFi Wallet

More Wallet Tips from a Pro

My cybersecurity pro really likes the soft wallet called SafePal for traders of any level of experience. SafePal has a hard wallet version, too. *Please, always download the soft wallets directly from the company* and then record all of your login information in your offline ledger. Double-check that you are using the correct URL. Since soft wallets as digital applications are more vulnerable to hacks, be mindful of the type and amount of cryptocurrency coins you will store there while you are in trader mode.

Soft Wallet Security Tips For Computer And Laptop Users

Make sure you have the actual soft wallet app URL, and bookmark that site on your computer so you can get to that site through the bookmark. You can also record that soft wallet URL on an offline ledger and copy and paste it from there. Either approach will make sure that you don't get misdirected down the wrong URL path!

If you opted to start right now, you can get your soft wallet up and running immediately, the apps are fast! Please order a hard wallet right away too.

Do not order hard wallets from Amazon or any other marketplace.
IMPORTANT: ONLY ORDER HARD WALLETS
DIRECTLY FROM THE MAKER'S WEBSITE

There have been a few instances where bad actors manipulate those devices by retaining the seed phrases so when a crypto newbie loads the wallet, the thieves are able to steal those funds using those same seed phrases. Forewarned is forearmed. My goal is that you stay vigilant and informed so that you're well-prepared.

I've found that it's relatively easy to transfer crypto from an exchange to a soft wallet, once you get the hang of it. Follow the instructions for transferring on that specific exchange and soft wallet. You'll need your receiving address for your soft wallet for that specific cryptocurrency that you're transferring. Each transaction involves sending from a specific sending address that's on the exchange. There is both a proper way and improper way to handle these transfers. Just like any new technology, transferring digital assets is confusing for the first few times. So, make sure you familiarize yourself thoroughly with the steps before transferring. Even better is to get support from your guide when you're first learning. You can lose money when it's done incorrectly. Remember my sad tale above.[11]

---

[11] *Here's a link to the resource section with examples of how to transfer coins and tokens: tamingcryptobook.com/resources*

STAGE FIVE: Time to Trade

By now, I'm banking that you're set up on an exchange. You've got your mad money sorted out, and now you're ready to acquire some cryptocurrency. What will you buy and what will you do with it once you have it?

Like buying high-quality stocks, some investors opt for the more expensive digital assets, like Bitcoin, because they like to buy and hold, banking on the belief that the value of Bitcoin will steadily climb over time. I think of those as the "buy and hold" coins. Those digital assets are ideal for storing on a hard wallet until you're ready to sell.

When someone trades cryptocurrencies, that means they are buying, selling, and/or swapping frequently, with the goal of taking short-term profits from changes in the values over short periods. That's like options trading.

For most trades on exchanges, a digital asset investor needs some ETH in order to trade. Because ETH is what's used to pay gas fees, without ETH, trades simply will not go through. That's why it's the ETH horses that pull the wagons for the FOMOs. They were the most robust horses, and without them, the wagons were stuck and could go nowhere.

My Stablecoin Strategy for Crypto Newbies

Remember how Freddie had the FOMOs acquire a good number of Tether ponies at the first auction house? Some they kept at their Soft

Wallet ranch to make trading easier along the trail. However, they also had a good number that they kept "on credit" at the auction house. That's what you can do. When you maintain a small amount of USDT Tether on an exchange as well as in your digital wallets, exchanges do not put a hold on trades which makes it poss transfer those digital assets immediately, unlike when you find trades with fiat currency.

Think of stablecoins as a neutral currency that functions as a bridge currency, providing a stable value and facilitating transactions while reducing value volatility for the investor, while enabling cross-border transfers. Stablecoins are cryptocurrencies whose value is stable and they are good for quick trading. They offer value consistency as well as the privacy and convenience offered by crypto transactions. USDT (Tether) is universally accepted on most exchanges and can be traded with several other types of crypto. (See trading pairs below.) Stablecoins often have low gas fees when you are buying, transferring, holding, or trading them.

> **SIDE NOTE**
>
> **A bridge currency is a digital currency that is used to help people exchange one type of cryptocurrency for another. It's like a middleman between the two currencies, making it easier for people to trade even if there isn't a direct way to do so.**

Trading Pairs: USDT/BTC

When you trade cryptocurrency, it's traded in pairs. That means that when you are on an exchange, you will identify which coins trade with which.

The combination of USDT and BTC is a popular trade (or swap). Let's use the USDT and BTC as an example and walk through this trading pair so you understand the process.

USDT is a stablecoin that's pegged to the U.S. dollar, which means it's always worth a dollar. It's a bridge cryptocurrency that's easy to swap and hedges against market value volatility. Keeping USDT in your wallets protects against market fluctuations while keeping you ready to swap and trade without facing restrictions that impact your ability to move your new digital assets to a digital wallet immediately.

BTC, Bitcoin, is the first and most well-known cryptocurrency. Like any cryptocurrency aside from stablecoins, its value fluctuates. Fun fact: BTC's price rose from just under $5,000 in March 2020 to over $63,000 in April 2021, only to drop in value to $30,000 in just two months.

This popular trading pair, USDT/BTC can be found on most major exchanges and trading platforms, so swapping between them is easy. This is also the case in reverse. That trading pair is written as BTC/USDT. Another popular trading pair is USDT/ETH and its reverse, ETH/USDT. The point is that having USDT ready to trade as a newbie positions you to trade and swap on any of the most popular exchanges directly without complications.

Due Diligence and Keeping Track

In the world of crypto trading, due diligence and being meticulous with your records pays off. This is where the importance of tracking your trades factors in. Accurate record-keeping helps you refine your trading strategies and makes tax filing easier. For each trade, record the specifics such as the date, the specific crypto asset traded, the amount, the price at which you bought or sold, the exchange on which the trade was executed, and the fees incurred. These data points will not only provide you with an overview of your portfolio's performance over time, but also highlight potential areas for improvement, including cost-effectiveness and timing of trades.

When it comes to transferring your crypto to your digital wallets, the type of cryptocurrency you have can often influence the strategy. Different cryptocurrencies have varying transaction speeds, network fees, and security levels, all of which can affect the decision-making process. For instance, Bitcoin transactions might be more secure but slower and costlier, which might prompt you to transfer large amounts in one go to minimize fees.

To send or receive cryptocurrencies, you use wallet addresses. A wallet address is akin to a bank account number—it's a unique identifier that points to your wallet and is used to receive funds. If you want to send crypto, you'll need the recipient's wallet receiving address. To receive any transfers, you'll provide your wallet receiving address to the sender.

Also, remember your hard and soft wallet strategies I mentioned when determining where to send the different types of crypto. Generally, my strategy is to send my stablecoins to the soft wallet for trading and to send my Bitcoin acquisitions to my hard wallet for more safe, secure, and long-term custody.

Here are some crypto accounting software options we found for portfolio tracking returns and data for tax purposes according to coinledger.io:

- **Best Portfolio tracker**: CoinStats
- **Best for investors looking to save money on taxes**: CoinLedger
- **Best for investors looking for detailed trade insights**: Delta
- **Best for investors looking for detailed market analysis**: CryptoCompare
- **Best for investors looking for manual trade entry**: CoinMarketCap
- **Best for investors looking for iPhone and Apple Watch functionality**: Crypto Pro
- **Best for investors looking to track all their assets in one place**: Kubera

STAGE SIX: Don't Get Misdirected – Best to Watch Your Steps

Almost from the start, ICO crypto exchange exit scams and "pump and dump" small-cap cryptocurrency schemes became the global white-collar crimes de jour. Criminals, and other unsavory types found themselves in the perfect storm for a financial feeding frenzy off of new prey. Digital euphoria had set in for investors, and establishing a new exchange was easy. Anyone with half a brain, a few technologists, and a good bit of sweet talk could entice impressionable, novice traders into "buying into" and trading on their exchanges. This kind of technological thievery was like stealing candy from a baby! OneCoin, PlexCoin, Shopin, Modern Tech, and so forth... many founders pulled off epic digital heists! Hundreds of millions were stolen while a few even faked their deaths. For some of these miscreant masterminds, the whereabouts of their bodies (dead or alive) remains a mystery! A few technical difficulties here, a couple hacks there, some misdirection from previously respected financial experts, and the investors' funds were history.

Dear Reader,
Remember how the FOMOs got so misdirected at Misdirection Mountain and lost several of their horses? The storm hit. The rug-puller bandits struck. The horses went crazy and Maverick was seriously injured, no longer able to guide them. Accidents don't discriminate. Anyone, anytime can get sideswiped. Circumstances will have us lose our focus and our way. Don't feel bad if you get misdirected. It happens to even the most savvy traders. Consider it a digital right of passage.

How To Get Back On Track
In the story, FOMO Junior saved them from further losses and devastation when he recognized that the compass, the map, and his Pigeon Phone

were not in sync. They were being led in the wrong direction! What can we learn from FOMO Junior?

1. Reassess the situation—how misdirected and off were they?
2. Take stock of the damage.
3. Plan out new action to get back on track.

When it comes to investments of *any* kind, bring yourself back to your goals and get back in the saddle by charting your new course.

Win or Lose, Keep Your Cool
Starting out, it's easy (and normal) to become seduced by the endless number of shiny object cryptocurrencies that are ripe for the taking. There are hordes of them (over 23,000 to be exact)! Think of FOMO Junior and his unicorn pony, Gumdrop. Unbeknownst to Junior, Gumdrop was a very risky buy that Maverick, as his guide, did not like. Initially, Gumdrop seemed healthy. But when the storm hit, Gumdrop succumbed to the elements, dying very quickly. He didn't have the strength to weather the storm. The same thing can happen to those of us new to crypto when we don't follow our plan, and instead get ahead of ourselves. If you find yourself feeling anxious, circle back to your goals. With any sort of investing, we can't control the factors that impact an asset's performance, but we can stay calm in the flurry of pricing highs and lows.

STAGE SEVEN: Safe at Home

My Hard Wallet Strategy: Bringing It Home

- Order your hard wallet
- Understand what your seed phrase does
- Safeguard your seed phrase
- Keep your own counsel when it comes to digital assets
- Transfer digital assets to your hard wallet
- Where will you keep it?
- Who else can access your digital assets if you need help?

The FOMO's second ranch was located in the Hard Wallet Ranch territory. Named the FOMO Family Ranch, their place was ideal for keeping their best horses more safe. It was difficult to reach, making it inconvenient for bandits to raid.

Your hard wallet is an <u>offline</u> physical storage device with a computer application component that you connect to your computer for transferring your coins and other digital assets to store. The hard wallets are optimal for storing digital assets for long periods. Since they are offline, they offer a higher level of security, unlike the soft wallets which are connected to the web 24/7. Even for small amounts, hardware wallets work well because they protect your private keys, and that makes for greater peace of mind than keeping crypto on an exchange or in a soft wallet.

Hard wallets can be purchased, whereas soft wallets are downloaded for free.

Coinbureau.com voted the following the best hard wallets for 2023:

- **Trezor Model T**, Coins supported: 1,000+
- **TLedger Nano X**, Coins supported: 1,800+
- **TNGRAVE ZERO**, Supported currencies: Bitcoin, Bitcoin Cash, Ethereum, Dash, Zcash, Litecoin, Binance Coin, XRP, Dogecoin, and Groestlcoin; also compatible with all ERC20 tokens
- **TELLIPAL** Titan, Coins supported: 46 Blockchains, 10,000+ coins and tokens

My cybersecurity pro endorses the Safepal hard wallet and finds it easy to navigate. At the risk of beating a dead horse (pun intended), whatever hard wallet you decide on, purchase it directly from the maker's website. Hard wallets generally cost between $100 and $200.

IMPORTANT: ONLY ORDER HARD WALLETS DIRECTLY FROM THE MAKER'S WEBSITE

Planting the Seed (Phrases)

A seed phrase, also known as a mnemonic seed phrase or a recovery phrase, currently might just be the single most important layer of security for crypto users. The seed phrase is used to back up and restore your wallets, ensuring access to your funds even if you lose your wallet's device or forget your password. A seed phrase acts as a master key to unlock access to a crypto wallet and is also the ultimate recovery tool for wallets on the blockchain. Computers can crash, phones get lost or broken, and hardware wallets can be forgotten, stolen, or destroyed. If any of these things happen, you will be happy to have your seed phrase safely tucked away. Some people write their hard wallet seed phrase on the back of their favorite family photo. Others keep an extra thumb drive in a safe-deposit box as a backup containing all of their passwords and seed phrases.

When you set up your crypto wallet (soft or hard), the wallet generates a seed phrase, which is a cluster of twelve, eighteen, or twenty-four random words. These words serve as a private key. To reiterate the seed phrase (AKA private key) can be used if you ever need to restore access to your funds. Best not take a picture of your seed phrases with your phone, as that will immediately put your seed phrases on the cloud. Better to connect a thumb drive to your computer and type in the seed phrases on the thumb drive's spreadsheet as well as noting them in a paper journal.

These words in your seed phrase are generated using a specific algorithm and need to be written down in the exact order they were provided. The order is as important as the words themselves. An example of a twelve-word recovery phrase is:

Stereo Fabric Lucky Avocado Trash Bench Beach Pillow Snake Citizen Void Again

Store your seed phrase securely, since anyone with access to it can gain control over your digital wallets. So again, let's deploy some old-school, lo-fi security measures, like your Excel ledger on the external thumb drive or a trusty pen and paper. Get your seed phrase down (in the proper order!) and store it safely so it can't fall into the wrong hands.

Best Practices for Seed Phrase Management

- Your seed phrases are the master keys to your digital assets, so only share with a trusted friend and/or adviser that will act on your behalf when you need them to. Decide now who that person is and how they will gain access to your passwords and seed phrases when that becomes important.
- Keep multiple physical copies of your seed phrases in secure and separate locations, such as in your safe-deposit box or a personal safe or even on the back of your favorite family photos!
- Keep your seed phrases off the cloud. Most apps on your devices are connected to the cloud, so don't keep them there.
- Consider using a metal backup solution, like a Cryptosteel or Billfold. These small, wallet-sized, stainless-steel enclosures are designed to protect any kind of crypto private key or recovery seed you may need from physical threats of destruction, like fires and floods.
- It's good practice to regularly verify the integrity of your stored seed phrase to ensure it remains legible and accessible in case you need to recover your wallet.

Mum's the Word!

To protect your crypto, keep your own counsel about what you are doing. That means don't talk about it, flaunt it, or display it. Set yourself up using the security measures I've written about in the book and find a good hiding place for your hard wallet. I have heard of people hiding their hard wallets in places like birdhouses, hollowed-out books, shoes, cereal boxes, even geocaching them in a specific location! Important to note: Wherever you keep your device, remember where the heck it is!

To Cash Out Or Not Cash Out Crypto—That Is The Question.

"Cashing out" means selling crypto coins or tokens in exchange for fiat money and then withdrawing the money to your bank account. Maybe you're ready to make a purchase with your earnings, or maybe you've come this far and crypto is just not for you. So how do you cash out? The process has gotten easier. You can use a crypto exchange and withdraw dollars (fiat), you can use an online broker, there are bitcoin ATM machines, and you can use a crypto debit card like Juno. Whichever way you go, remember to look at fees and record the transactions for any taxes. And review your goals before cashing out or selling your crypto.

Wrapping It Up: From FOMO to Savvy and Prepared—What's Next?

Your saddle has been broken in some. You're no longer a crypto newbie! Time to choose what's next. I'm hoping this book has helped you tame your FOMO and show you that, with a solid approach, being mindful, and applying knowledge, you can strategically venture into the Wild West of crypto. So, where do you fall?

- Do you want to continue to investigate and learn?
- Are you ready to lightly dip your toes in the crypto water?
- Are you seeing the potential of becoming a student of the crypto space and turning it into a side gig or career?

What's next for you is for you to choose. If you would like to get started, here are some beginning strategies to consider.

Strategies To Consider

- Are you interested in dollar-cost averaging, which is securing smaller amounts at regular intervals over time?
- Do you prefer to buy one and done?
- Do you like being more diversified with more than one digital asset?

Food for Thought: "Long-term" means something different in the crypto space.
Traditionally, assets are given a "window" of time, between one, five, ten, and even twenty years, to ripen. Cryptocurrencies are distinctly different. They can come into their own in six months to five years.

Your strategies will dictate how you invest. Before getting on the trail, the FOMOs had a plan to trade horses on the frontier and found some good opportunities to do that. Buying and then selling higher (or lower) by a predetermined percentage is a strategy that many use for locking in returns. Rather than reacting negatively to these unstable bear markets, falling prices provide more opportunities to generate returns. These strategies take some education, certain tools, and a bit of practice, but once you learn them, they can be applied to more than the crypto market. No need to feel driven to predict the market. You're better off knowing a few strategies you can use so that whatever happens, you know what action to take that will add coin to your sugar bowl.

Some digital asset investors like to use what are called "stop losses" when they acquire a coin. A stop loss is an order you put in on a crypto exchange for selling a coin if it falls below a certain price. This strategy either locks in profits or migates losses. Of course the trader is then faced with the question of when to buy in again for that coin or another. Since the market can't be timed, I think that somewhere this approach falls between gambling and speculation. I say that because you'll either be guessing or using a different strategy to align with how the market seems to be behaving. Becoming savvy around investing in digital assets takes understanding and putting into practice a few strategies that will allow you to determine how you'll play the crypto game.

I am not a financial advisor and I'm not advising or directing you on the approach or plan that makes the most sense for you. My goal has been to provide you with some basic concepts to help you on your digital asset investment journey. Here are four strategies that seasoned digital asset traders put to use:

- Dollar-cost averaging (getting a bit as you go).
- The 5% strategy.
- Reset your digital assets and pull out your original principal.
- Using stop losses to lock in profits and/or ward off extreme losses.

Dollar-Cost Averaging Dollar-cost averaging is a great way to slowly acquire the same digital asset over time because you're trading in regular intervals. It's what the FOMOs did when they bought the same type of horses at both auction houses. The horses' values varied, but it didn't impact them negatively because the price paid per horse averaged out over time. In the end, their stables were full of the horses they needed for their ranch to expand, which was their bigger goal after securing the ranch.

The 5 Percent Strategy for Taking Small Profits

By establishing the goal of a five percent profit on a coin, when you secure that coin, you can then organize to trade that coin once it hits that 5 percent return mark. Even if the value of the coin surpasses 5 percent, it ought not have you change how you approach the strategy. Five percent profit is profit! There's no place for FOMO when it comes to being in the black in crypto.

If you let it get under your skin, the quick rise and fall of cryptocurrency markets can make an average crypto fan nuts! Day traders like to watch the market every day. As a digital asset investor, I don't day trade. I like to set alerts for the coins via the app called CRYPTOCURRENCY ALERTING (https://cryptocurrencyalerting.com). This app alerts a trader when the coin is close to a swap price and sends a prompt to put in a swap order. Use alerts to stay focused on the goal you set for profiting and managing your digital assets.

Reset Your Digital Assets and Pull Out Your Original Principal

For those of you who have acquired altcoins as well as ETH and BTC, a leading expert in the crypto space that I follow recommends swapping those altcoins back to USDT or USDC (stablecoins) twice a year or so. The purpose is to "reset" the altcoin digital assets by taking them out of the market while pulling out principal, the first money you put in. This strategy is used to safekeep your original money in, help you stay in profit, and lets you check the pulse of the market so you can choose if you want to stay with those same altcoins or change direction. (Reminder: As with any swap, keep track of the swaps for tax purposes depending on your country's tax laws.)

Using Stop Losses to Protect Your Digital Asset Gains
Since crypto prices are more unruly than a bucking bronco, crypto traders will use stop losses to make sure their profits don't get derailed. A stop loss is a trader's tool that can be used on exchanges to automatically sell a cryptocurrency should it hit a predetermined price. It puts you in control to limit price declines by triggering a sell order if prices fall below a certain point.

Here are the steps involved in setting a stop loss order on an exchange.
1. You've chosen the coin and swapped for it at a price.
2. You set a target price for selling (example, 5 percent over cost).
3. You decide how much of a price drop you can stomach (example, 10 percent lower than cost).
4. For anything under that price, you select the stop loss order option on the crypto exchange.

Because crypto's volatility tends to exceed what we see with popular stocks, if you want to actively track any specific coin's activity, you can always set an alert for that coin to notify you if the coin is getting close to that stop loss order number. Stop losses can always be adjusted as long as they haven't been triggered.

Conclusion

Dear Reader,

You've made your way across the new frontier! The seven steps served the FOMO family on their journey. I trust your seven steps have been helpful for you too. I've done my best to give you a relatively simplified approach for entering the very complicated crypto space safely, with strategies that will help you profit quickly. If there's anything you take from your read of this book, staying safe and setting yourself up well for the long run takes top billing. After all, at this stage of DeFi, you are in charge of your security and facilitating correct transfers of crypto funds. Whether it's your identity or your digital assets, this new digital world is calling for every one of us to do more to take security into our own hands. As much as surprise attacks from hackers can't be stopped, we can make it much more difficult for them to find us with a few simple actions.

So, take one step at a time as you develop your crypto skills. The trail will likely have forks, boulders, twists, and turns. Build your competencies as you ride along. The FOMOs did themselves a disservice when they celebrated at the saloon a bit too early, then got hit with that terrible storm. It's always better to be prepared and move slowly than rush ahead and find yourself teetering on the edge of a financial cliff that you did not see.

Be resolute in your goals but stay nimble in how you go after them. The FOMOs focused on finding their Hard Wallet ranch. You'll become a better rider as you journey toward your destination, whether that's becoming a capable digital asset investor or remaining an informed crypto-curious observer.

No need to go it alone. Consider locating and working with worthy guides. The FOMOs had Maverick and Freddie. Seek out Mavericks of your own.

As we finish here, do a gut check. How committed are you to your aims? As someone completely new to digital asset investing, you'll be heading into a few new frontiers—blockchain technology, the cryptocurrency markets, and working inside the scope of your risk tolerance and timeline for achieving your goals. For those of you who are unfamiliar with modern technology, simply becoming aware of the basics of crypto might just be what you're ready for. That was me until I prepared myself to become a student of blockchain. For others, this primer has the potential to be a launchpad into a whole new future.

Ultimately, the optimal timing for entering the DeFi (decentralized finance) frontier is personal, because as I see it, blockchain is still its own version of the Wild West. For many younger, computer competent individuals, working with crypto wallets and managing their digital assets takes minimal effort. Your personal circumstances will tell you what next step is right to take.

Whether you choose to venture into the new digital frontier or simply read about it, my intention is that you choose knowledge over fear. I do foresee that blockchain technology will continue to birth many exciting and worthwhile opportunities for all of us. As for which digital assets will stand the test of time in the decentralized economy, it's hard to say. As this new digital technology becomes integrated into the systems of our society, having the base knowledge presented here might support you into feeling more confident and be more agile around adapting to a new digital world. Keep going! Every new step will draw you closer to becoming a savvy digital investor. Here's to new beginnings!

Afterword: Can Crypto Be Tamed?

You and I can't tame crypto, but governments might be able to.

Look back in history at how the United States took control of the Wild West. It could only be a matter of time before governments contain this frontier too. The jury's still out. As of June 2023, eleven countries including the U.S. are introducing centralized digital coins into their monetary systems, and forty more are in line to do the same. These coins are created by the countries' federal reserve banks or central banks and are distinct from (are not) decentralized cryptocurrencies. In the United States, these new coins are known as centralized bank digital coins (CBDC).

So, when the CBDCs of the world enter the money supply, what will happen with the decentralized cryptocurrencies? Will the DeFi economy expand or contract? Will DeFi have a rightful place in the global economy? What will become the norm, and what will fall away? Time will tell, but economic systems are always evolving, and that we can count on.[12]

RESOURCES

Please see our resources page for additional links, case studies, definitions, assessments, and information:
tamingcryptobook.com/resources

Glossary[13]

Adaptive scaling: Adaptive scaling for mining in cryptocurrencies means that the computer system that runs the cryptocurrency adjusts how hard it is to "mine" or create new coins based on how many people are trying to do it. If lots of people are trying to mine, the system makes it harder to do, so that not too many coins are created too quickly. If fewer people are mining, the system makes it easier so that enough coins are created. This helps keep the system working properly and makes sure that everyone can use the cryptocurrency fairly.

Algorithm: An algorithm for crypto, which is short for cryptography, is like a secret code-making recipe that computers use to keep information safe and secure. Imagine you have a secret message you want to send to your friend, but you don't want anyone else to read it. The algorithm would be like a set of instructions telling you how to change the letters in your message into a crazy mix of letters, numbers, and symbols that nobody can understand. Then, only your friend, who knows the special steps (or has a secret key) to change it back, can read the secret message. This is super important for things like protecting passwords, online shopping, and keeping personal information private on the internet.

Altcoin: An altcoin, short for "alternative coin," is any cryptocurrency other than Bitcoin. These coins are alternatives to Bitcoin and often have slightly different features or functions. Examples of altcoins include Ethereum, Litecoin, and Ripple. They can be created by forking an existing blockchain, creating a new one, or rebranding an existing one. They are different from Bitcoin in terms of algorithm, mining process, and many other factors.

Bear Market: Bear markets occur when stock prices fall 20 percent or more for a sustained period of time in periods of economic slowdown and higher unemployment. Investors often make emotional sell decisions in bear markets by selling off assets.

Blockchain: Blockchain is an autonomous digital record-keeping technology designed to capture and store dealings securely, transparently, and in a way that prevents tampering. This technology essentially functions as a database dispersed over a network of interconnected nodes. Each node within the network maintains an identical copy of this database and observes the same record of transactions. Transaction data is registered within 'blocks,' which are interlinked through cryptographic methods, leading to the term 'blockchain.' While its most popular application is in the field of cryptocurrencies, it can also be leveraged in numerous other contexts, including the management of supply chains, the operation of voting systems, and the verification of digital identities.

Bridge Cryptocurrency: A bridge currency is a digital currency used to help people exchange one type of cryptocurrency for another. It's like a middleman between the two currencies, making it easier for people to

[12] See tamingcryptobook.com/resources

trade when there isn't a direct way to do so. Popular examples of a bridge currency are Tether (USDT) and Bitcoin (BTC).

Bull Market: Bull markets occur when investment prices are on the rise for sustained periods. Driven by thriving economies and low unemployment that commonly come with bull markets, investors are eager to buy or hold onto securities.

CeFi (centralized finance): CeFi is a financial system or platform that is centralized, meaning it is owned and operated by a single entity or authority. In CeFi, a central entity has control over the financial system, including the management of user funds, execution of transactions, and decision-making processes. Examples of CeFi platforms include traditional banks, stock exchanges, and centralized cryptocurrency exchanges. CeFi platforms offer regulatory compliance, ease of use, and customer support, but may also have drawbacks such as the potential for censorship, lack of transparency, and centralization risks.

Crypto Airdrop: A crypto airdrop is a marketing strategy where Web3 start-ups directly deposit digital tokens into the wallets of active blockchain community members as a gift.

Cryptocurrency: Crypto is a term that is short for "cryptocurrency," which refers to digital or virtual currencies that use cryptography for security. Cryptocurrencies are decentralized and are not controlled by any government or financial institution. Instead, they use complex mathematical algorithms to verify and record transactions on a public ledger called a blockchain.

Cryptocurrency Assessing Value: Assessing the value of a cryptocurrency involves analysis and intuition, as there is no single metric or formula that can accurately predict the value of a cryptocurrency. Investors and traders need to consider a range of factors and make their own informed decisions based on their individual risk tolerance, timeframes, and investment goals. Here are a few factors to consider to evaluate a cryptocurrency's potential value..

- *Market Demand*: The market demand is the level of demand for a particular cryptocurrency. Factors that can influence demand include the popularity of the cryptocurrency, the number of users and developers supporting it, and its perceived utility and value proposition.

- *Technology and Innovation*: The technology behind a cryptocurrency can impact its value, as newer and more innovative technologies may be perceived as more valuable and have a greater potential for growth.

- *Security and Trustworthiness*: The level of security and trustworthiness of a cryptocurrency can also impact its value because

---

[13]*Definitions generated or vetted by ChatGPT, 2023, OpenAI, https://chat.openai.com. Rewritten for style and content.*

cryptocurrencies that are secure and considered trustworthy are more likely to be supported by investors and users.

- *Adoption and Use Cases*: The level of adoption and the number of real-world uses for a cryptocurrency can also impact its value. Cryptocurrencies that are widely used and accepted are likely to be more valuable than those that are not.

- *Competition and Market Trends*: The competitive landscape and market trends can impact cryptocurrency, as new projects and market shifts can change the overall market dynamics and impact the perceived value of existing cryptocurrencies.

- *Cryptocurrency by Category*: payment crypto, privacy crypto, security crypto, legal crypto, fintech crypto, utility crypto, stablecoin crypto, platform crypto, bridge crypto.

Cryptocurrency Components: Cryptocurrencies are made up of a combination of technological, cryptographic, and financial components that work together to create a decentralized, secure, and transparent system for storing and transferring value, including:

- *Blockchain Technology*: Facilitates the operation of digital currencies. It's a dispersed ledger system that chronicles and safeguards all dealings securely and transparently.

- *Cryptography*: This refers to the techniques and algorithms used to secure and protect the transactions and user identities on the blockchain.

- *Mining or Validation Mechanism*: This is the process by which transactions are verified and added to the blockchain. Depending on the type of cryptocurrency, this process can involve proof of work (PoW), proof of stake (PoS), or other consensus mechanisms.

- *Digital Wallets*: These are digital tools used to store and manage cryptocurrencies and can be either software- or hardware-based.

- *Tokens or Coins*: These are the digital assets that represent cryptocurrency and can be bought, sold, and traded on various exchanges. They are also used as a means of payment and value transfer within the cryptocurrency ecosystem.

Cryptography: Cryptography is the science of keeping information secure and has been used for centuries to protect secrets. It involves transforming plain text (regular words and numbers) into a coded form called ciphertext, which can only be understood by someone who has the key to decode it. Cryptography is an essential tool for privacy, security, and confidentiality, and with the advent of computers and the internet, it has become increasingly important for securing electronic communication and data storage.

Cryptography Encryption Methods: Each method has its own strengths and weaknesses, and the choice of encryption method depends on the specific application and security requirements.

- *Symmetric-Key Encryption*: In this method, the same key is used for both encryption and decryption and is kept secret between the sender and receiver. Examples of symmetric-key encryption algorithms include advanced encryption standard (AES), data encryption standard (DES), and triple DES (3DES).

- *Asymmetric-Key Encryption*: This method uses a duo of keys—a public key, which can be publicly shared, and a private key, which is maintained secretly—for the purpose of encrypting and decrypting data. Data encrypted with a public key can exclusively be decoded with its matching private key, and the inverse is also true. Protocols like RSA and Elliptic Curve Cryptography (ECC) are examples of encryption methods that utilize this two-key system.

- *Hash*: Hash functions are like one-way streets that turn a message or a file into a set length of symbols, known as a hash. The output is typically a string of characters that represents the input in a unique way. Hash functions are used for data integrity and digital signatures and are often used in combination with other encryption methods. Examples of hash functions include SHA-256 and MD5.

- *Steganography*: This method involves hiding a secret message within a larger message or file so that the existence of the secret message is concealed. For example, a message could be hidden within the pixels of an image or within the audio track of a video. Even though steganography does not inherently represent an encryption method, it's frequently employed alongside encryption to bolster security levels.

Crypto Winter: Crypto winter is a term used to describe a prolonged bear market in the cryptocurrency industry. It refers to a period of time when the overall value of cryptocurrencies and the crypto market as a whole experience a significant decline in value, often accompanied by a decrease in trading volume, investment, and public interest.

Decentralized Applications (dApps): Decentralized applications, or dApps, are applications that are built on top of blockchain networks and operate in a decentralized manner, meaning they do not rely on a central authority or server to function. Instead, they are powered by smart contracts and operate in a trustless manner, where transactions are validated by a network of nodes rather than a single entity. Examples of dApps include decentralized exchanges, prediction markets, and social networks.

Decentralized Autonomous Organization (DAO): A DAO is a decentralized organization that operates through smart contracts on a blockchain network, such as Ethereum. In a DAO, decision-making processes and management functions are automated through smart contracts, which are executed based on predetermined rules and conditions. DAOs enable stakeholders to participate in the decision-making process and governance of the organization through the use of tokens or voting rights. DAOs have the potential to operate autonomously, transparently, and efficiently, without the need for intermediaries or central authorities. However, DAOs may also face challenges, such as smart contract vulnerabilities and regulatory compliance.

Decentralized Finance (DeFi): DeFi is a system of financial applications and protocols that operate on a decentralized blockchain network, such as Ethereum. In DeFi, there is no central authority or entity controlling the financial system, and transactions are executed through smart contracts. Examples of DeFi platforms include decentralized exchanges (DEXs), lending and borrowing protocols, and stablecoins. DeFi offers several advantages, including decentralization, transparency, and accessibility, but also has some drawbacks, such as the potential for smart contract vulnerabilities and liquidity risks.

Exchange: A cryptocurrency exchange, also known as a digital currency platform (DCE), is an enterprise that facilitates the trading of digital or cryptocurrencies for other forms of value, such as traditional currency or different digital currencies. These marketplaces may accommodate various payment methods, like credit card transactions, bank transfers, or other forms of remuneration, in return for digital or cryptocurrencies. Well-known examples of such platforms include Coinbase, Kraken, and Binance.

Exit Scam: In the realm of digital currencies, an exit scam refers to the act where those marketing a cryptocurrency abscond with the investors' funds during or following an initial coin offering (ICO). This practice typically encompasses the initiators launching a novel cryptocurrency platform, promoting the currency and its ideology, attracting investment, possibly operating the enterprise for a brief period, and then vanishing with the collected funds, leaving the project deserted.

Fiat Money: Fiat currency is a variety of monetary unit that is sanctioned by the government and doesn't rely on tangible assets like gold for its value. The American dollar, the European euro, and the British pound exemplify forms of fiat currency.

Fintech Crypto: Fintech crypto refers to cryptocurrencies that are designed specifically for use in the financial technology (fintech) industry. These cryptocurrencies are typically used for fast and secure cross-border transactions between financial institutions and are often designed to be more efficient and cost-effective than traditional payment methods. Examples of fintech cryptocurrencies include Ripple and Stellar..

Fork: A fork occurs when a blockchain network splits into two separate paths or versions of the blockchain, typically due to a change in the rules or protocol of the network.

- *Hard Fork*: A hard fork occurs when, due to a change in the rules or protocol, there is a permanent divergence in the blockchain that is not backward-compatible with the previous version of the blockchain. This means that any nodes that continue to operate on the old version will no longer be able to participate in the network. This can result in a new cryptocurrency being created, with its own separate blockchain.

• *Soft Fork*: A soft fork arises when an adjustment to the regulations or protocol of the blockchain is implemented in a way that's compatible with its prior version. Consequently, nodes operating on the older version of the blockchain can maintain their network participation. However, they won't be capable of utilizing any fresh features or functionalities introduced in the updated version.

Fork Reasons: Common reasons why forks develop in cryptocurrencies are:

- *Changes To The Consensus Mechanism*: If there are changes made to the way transactions are validated, such as a change in the proof of work or proof of stake algorithms, it can result in a fork.

- *Disagreements Within The Community*: Differences of opinion among developers, miners, users, or other stakeholders can lead to a split in the network, resulting in a fork.

- *Technical Upgrades*: If there are upgrades to the network's software that are not backward-compatible with the previous version, it can result in a fork.

- *Scaling Issues*: If the network is experiencing congestion due to a high volume of transactions, it may need to implement changes to its block size or transaction processing times. These changes can result in a fork.

- *Security Concerns*: If there are security vulnerabilities discovered in the network's software, it may need to implement changes to address the issue. These changes can result in a fork.

- *Governance Issues*: If there are disputes over how the network should be governed or operated, it can lead to a fork.

- *Fork Example*: A fork occurs when a blockchain network splits into two separate paths or versions of the blockchain, typically due to a change in the rules or protocol of the network. There are two kinds of forks: At the time, Bitcoin was facing congestion due to a high volume of transactions, which led to slow transaction times and high fees. The community was divided on how to address this issue, with some advocating for a larger block size limit and others proposing alternative solutions. When a consensus could not be reached, a group of developers and miners decided to fork the Bitcoin network and create Bitcoin Cash, which had a larger block size limit of 8 MB compared to Bitcoin's 1 MB limit. This change allowed for faster transaction times and lower fees on the Bitcoin Cash network. As a result of the fork, Bitcoin Cash became a separate cryptocurrency with its own blockchain and community of users. While Bitcoin and Bitcoin Cash share a common history, they are now separate entities with their own unique features and characteristics.

Gas Fee: A gas fee is a transaction fee on the Ethereum blockchain network. According to Ethereum's developer pages, gas is "the fuel that allows the Ethereum network to operate, in the same way that a car needs gasoline to run." Other cryptocurrencies may simply call these transaction fees, miner fees, or something similar. However, since Ethereum is currently the second-largest crypto by market cap, the term "gas" is often applied when referring to the fees involved in executing work on other blockchains.

Getting Off Zero: A concept used in the cryptocurrency and blockchain industry that refers to the process of an individual or organization acquiring their first crypto asset or making their first cryptocurrency transaction. "Getting off zero" can also be used in a broader context to refer to the process of adopting a new technology or entering a new market. The term emphasizes the importance of taking the first step toward utilizing cryptocurrencies and blockchain technology, which can lead to increased adoption, awareness, and potential benefits.

Know Your Customer (KYC): KYC (or KYC check) refers to the process of verifying that your customer is who they say they are and can also involve establishing that a potential client meets investor requirements for that financial entity.

Legal Crypto: Legal crypto refers to blockchain-based platforms that are designed to facilitate legal transactions, such as property transfers or ticket sales, in a secure, efficient, and transparent manner. These platforms leverage the immutability and transparency of blockchain technology to provide a more trustworthy and efficient way of executing legal transactions. Examples of legal cryptocurrencies include Aventus and Propy..

Market Capitalization: "Market capitalization," or "market cap," plays a critical role in assessing cryptocurrencies as it offers a valuation estimate of a specific digital currency's total worth in the market. This is determined by multiplying the existing price of the digital currency by the total supply of its coins or tokens. There are several reasons why market cap holds significance. Firstly, it offers an insight into the size and acceptance of a cryptocurrency, assisting investors in gauging the interest in a specific project. Secondly, it allows for the comparison of various digital currencies to evaluate their comparative worth and potential for expansion. Lastly, market cap can influence a cryptocurrency's liquidity and stability - higher market cap coins usually see larger trade volumes and are less prone to price fluctuations. In summary, market cap is a crucial consideration for investors and traders in their analysis of digital currencies.

Metaverse: The metaverse is like a giant, online playground where you can create a character, called an avatar, to represent yourself and interact with other people's characters and the virtual world around you. Imagine combining video games, social media, and virtual reality into one big space on the internet where your character can hang out with friends, go to virtual concerts, build houses, or even attend school. It's like taking all the cool things you can do on the internet and putting them into a 3D world that feels almost like real life, but with endless possibilities to create and explore without leaving your computer or headset.

Minable Cryptocurrencies: Minable cryptocurrencies are digital assets that can be mined using a proof of work (PoW) algorithm. This procedure requires resolving intricate mathematical puzzles to authenticate transactions and generate new blocks within the blockchain. As miners solve these mathematical problems, they are rewarded with a certain amount of the cryptocurrency as an incentive.

Mining: Mining for other cryptocurrencies is like a big math competition where you use your computer to solve really tough equations. When you solve one of these equations, you get a small prize in the form of some of that cryptocurrency. Miners use their computers to process and verify transactions on the blockchain, and, in return, they get a small amount of that cryptocurrency as a reward. Different cryptocurrencies have different methods of mining. The most common is "proof of work." Note: not all crypto is mined, some are pre-mined (see pre-mined).

Mining Types: There a few different methods of crypto mining (creation). Here are the most common:

- *Proof of Work (PoW)*: This is the most common method of mining, where participants, much like Bitcoin miners, vie to unravel intricate mathematical puzzles to verify transactions and append new blocks to the blockchain. The miner who first solves the puzzle is granted a specified quantity of the respective digital currency.

- *Proof of Stake (PoS)*: This method of mining involves staking a certain amount of the cryptocurrency in order to validate transactions and add new blocks to the blockchain. The amount of cryptocurrency staked determines the miner's chances of being chosen to validate a block, and the miner is rewarded with a certain amount of the cryptocurrency.

- *Cloud Mining*: This type of mining involves renting mining power from a company that operates mining hardware on behalf of its customers. The customer pays a fee in exchange for a share of the mining rewards.

- *Solo Mining*: This type of mining is where the miner uses their own resources to mine, without joining a pool. It is more difficult and less profitable, but in the end, the miner will have the full rewards to themselves.

- *Pooled Mining*: This is where miners combine their resources to mine together as a group. They share the rewards proportionally to their contributed hash rate.

Some examples of minable cryptocurrencies include Bitcoin, Ethereum, and Litecoin. Mining requires significant computational power, which can be provided by specialized hardware such as ASICs (application specific integrated circuits) or GPUs (graphics processing units).

Node: A node is like one special computer that is part of a big team of computers. This team of computers works together to make sure that all the transactions made using cryptocurrency are safe and fair. Each node has a copy of a special book called the ledger, where all the transactions are recorded, and the nodes work together to make sure that the information in the book is accurate and nobody can cheat.

Non-Fungible Token (NFT): An NFT, or Non-Fungible Token, is a unique form of digital property authenticated via blockchain technology, usually the Ethereum blockchain. Distinct from fungible tokens like cryptocurrencies, NFTs are not interchangeable on a like-for-like basis, given their distinct properties, metadata, and records of ownership. NFTs can embody various types of digital assets, ranging from digital art, music, videos, to virtual real estate, and can be bought, sold, or traded on platforms specialized for NFT transactions. Particularly in the realm of art, NFTs have emerged as a popular trend, empowering artists to profit from their digital works and offering purchasers a verified proof of authenticity and ownership.

Non-minable: Non-minable cryptocurrencies are digital assets that cannot be mined using a PoW (proof of work) algorithm. Instead, these cryptocurrencies are often pre-mined or created through alternative means, such as an initial coin offering (ICO). Non-minable cryptocurrencies are usually based on a proof of stake (PoS) or proof of authority (PoA) algorithm, which involves validating transactions based on the number of coins held by the validator, rather than through computational power. Some examples of non-minable cryptocurrencies are Cardano, Ripple, and Stellar Lumens. These cryptocurrencies are validated by validators who hold a certain amount of the cryptocurrency and are incentivized through rewards for their participation.

Payment Crypto: Cryptos for payment, often referred to as payment cryptocurrencies, are digital currencies principally employed to facilitate transactions or payments among individuals or businesses. These digital currencies are engineered to provide quick, secure, and economical alternatives to conventional methods of payment, including bank transfers or credit card transactions. Bitcoin and Litecoin stand as examples of such payment cryptocurrencies.

Permission-Less: Inside of the decentralized model of transacting with cryptocurrencies, permission-less refers to an open and transparent system where anyone, autonomously, can participate without needing approval from a central authority or intermediary, like a bank. Examples of cryptocurrencies that operate as permission-less coins are Bitcoin, Ethereum, and Litecoin.

Platform Crypto: Cryptos serving as platforms, or platform cryptocurrencies, offer a foundation on which developers can construct decentralized applications (dApps) on an underlying blockchain network. These digital currencies are structured to allow developers to initiate and implement smart contracts and dApps, which can operate independently and with transparency, negating the need for any intermediaries. These platform-centric cryptocurrencies also commonly facilitate payments for transaction fees and computational resources within the system. Ethereum and Cardano are instances of such platform cryptocurrencies.

Pre-Mined: Pre-mined cryptocurrency refers to a digital currency category wherein a specified quantity of coins or tokens are generated and disseminated to particular individuals or groups prior to the cryptocurrency becoming accessible to the public. This indicates that a certain portion of the total supply is already in circulation before the official introduction of the cryptocurrency. The initial recipients of these coins or tokens are typically the cryptocurrency's inventors or other insiders. XRP serves as an instance of a pre-mined cryptocurrency, initially established in 2012 with a static supply of 100 billion coins.

Privacy Crypto: Privacy crypto refers to cryptocurrencies that prioritize the privacy and anonymity of users and transactions. These cryptocurrencies use various techniques, such as encryption and obfuscation, to obscure transaction details, such as sender and recipient addresses, as well as the amount of cryptocurrency being transacted. Examples of privacy cryptocurrencies include Monero and Zcash.

Private Key: A private key is a confidential numerical and alphabetical sequence that grants a user the ability to control and transact their digital assets. It's a unique identifier that is exclusively known by the cryptocurrency wallet's owner and is employed for transferring and managing cryptocurrency. The private key's safekeeping is crucial in maintaining ownership of one's digital assets, as its security prevents unauthorized individuals from accessing the wallet's content.

Private Key Sample: Private keys can vary in length and format depending on the cryptocurrency and wallet used, but they are always unique and known only to the individual who created the wallet. This is an example of a private key for a Bitcoin wallet: 5KJvsngHeMpm884wtkJNzQGaCErckhHJBGFsvd3VyK5qMZXj3hS.

Private Ledger: A private ledger is a type of distributed ledger technology (DLT) where access to the ledger is restricted to a specific group of participants or entities. Unlike public ledgers, where anyone can participate and view the transactions on the network, private ledgers are designed for a closed group of participants who trust one another and have a need to share information and record transactions securely. Private ledgers therefore offer greater privacy, control, and security than public ledgers. Private ledgers are often used in enterprise blockchain applications where privacy and confidentiality are critical, such as supply chain management, financial services, and healthcare.

Public Key: A public key is used to receive cryptocurrency payments into a digital wallet. It is part of a public-private key pair and is shared publicly with others to receive cryptocurrency payments. The public key is a critical component of cryptocurrency ownership and is used to identify the wallet and receive cryptocurrency payments. Here is an example of a public key for a Bitcoin wallet: 1A1zP1eP5QGefi2DMPTfTL5SLmv7DivfNa. This is a randomly generated string of letters and numbers that is unique to this Bitcoin wallet. Other cryptocurrencies may use different formats for their public keys, but they are always a unique code that is used to receive cryptocurrency payments into a wallet.

Public Ledger: A public ledger, in the context of cryptocurrency, is an openly accessible database that maintains all transaction records on a specific crypto network. This system, decentralized and transparent in nature, isn't under the control of a single entity, enabling all transactions to be inspected and verified by anyone with ledger access. Every transaction, referred to as a "block," is ratified by a network of nodes that are scattered across the network. After verification, each block is appended to the blockchain - a sequence of blocks arranged in chronological order, encapsulating the entire history of network transactions. Public ledgers provide several advantages to cryptocurrencies, including transparency, security, and permanence. Given its decentralized and distributed architecture, it's exceedingly difficult for any individual or group to tamper or alter the ledger, ensuring secure transactions and the network's integrity.

Pump and Dump: Pump-and-dump schemes are a type of crypto scam also known as a "rug pull." These scams involve market manipulators who spread false information about a crypto project and eventually sell their tokens (or "pull the rug") after enough retail investors buy into the currency.

ReceivingAddress: A receiving address in the context of cryptocurrency is a unique series of letters and numbers utilized for receiving cryptocurrency transactions. This address is produced by a user's cryptocurrency wallet and is exclusive to the user's account. When cryptocurrency is sent to this address, the transaction is documented on the blockchain, visible to anyone in the network. It's crucial to differentiate between receiving addresses and private keys - the latter is utilized for accessing and handling the cryptocurrency assets linked to the respective address. For each transaction, a new receiving address should ideally be generated to bolster security and ensure privacy..

Rug Pull: A "rug pull" is a crypto scam in which defrauders lie to the public to attract funding and quickly run off with investors' digital tokens..

Security Crypto: "Security crypto" refers to cryptocurrencies that are primarily designed to provide security to blockchain networks and their associated applications. These cryptocurrencies are used to secure the blockchain network against various types of attacks and to maintain the integrity of the blockchain data. Examples of security cryptocurrencies include Chainlink and Polkadot.

Sending Address: An alphanumeric code that is used to initiate a cryptocurrency transaction. A sending address is associated with the cryptocurrency wallet of the user who is sending the transaction. When initiating a transaction, the user enters the receiving address of the recipient, along with the amount of cryptocurrency they wish to send. The sending address is used to sign the transaction and record it on the blockchain. It is important to note that sending addresses are not to be confused with private keys, which are used to authorize the transaction and access the cryptocurrency funds associated with the sending address.

Sending addresses should be kept secure to prevent unauthorized access to the wallet.

Smart Contract: A smart contract is a set of rules written in computer code that automatically executes when certain conditions are met. For example, a smart contract could be used to automatically give a piggy bank to a little brother on his fifteenth birthday. In the same way, smart contracts on the Ethereum network can be used for a variety of purposes, like managing a digital store or creating a legal contract between parties..

Stablecoin: Stablecoin denotes a category of cryptocurrency that is tethered to a more stable asset like the U.S. dollar or gold to ensure a constant value. These coins are often employed to transfer assets between diverse cryptocurrency exchanges or to conduct transactions without the inherent price volatility seen in other cryptocurrencies. Some common stablecoins are Tether and USD Coin.

Staking: Staking involves securing or confining cryptocurrency tokens as collateral to aid the functionality of a blockchain network, and in turn, receive rewards. In the context of a proof of stake (PoS) blockchain network, staking means retaining a specified number of cryptocurrency tokens as collateral to become a validator or a node on the network. These validators take on the responsibility of processing and authenticating transactions on the blockchain, and for their services, they are compensated with fresh cryptocurrency tokens or transaction charges. Staking is a prevalent method for cryptocurrency owners to gain a passive income from their holdings while concurrently supporting the operations of a blockchain network. Nevertheless, staking often requires a minimal quantity of cryptocurrency to be staked, and it may involve risks, such as the potential loss of staked tokens if the network is breached.

Swapping: "Swapping" is a term used to refer to the exchange of one cryptocurrency for another. Swapping can occur on a variety of platforms, including centralized cryptocurrency exchanges, decentralized exchanges (DEXs), and automated market makers (AMMs). Swapping typically involves selecting the cryptocurrency pair to trade, specifying the amount to be exchanged, and confirming the transaction. Swapping can occur at market rates, or the user may set their own price based on market conditions. Swapping is often used as a way to diversify cryptocurrency holdings, take advantage of market opportunities, or convert one cryptocurrency to another for specific uses or applications.

Token: A token serves as a form of digital value unit which can be applied for numerous tasks online. Just as traditional currencies, tokens can be utilized for procuring items, accessing specific services, or funding ventures on the internet. Furthermore, they can act as proof of ownership, such as in the case of a token demonstrating one's right to a digital collectible (referred to as an NFT), or securitized tokens that stand for equity in a corporation. These tokens are safely stored in a virtual wallet, from where they can be transferred to others or received, similar to how digital communication like emails or texts works. The role of tokens is crucial as they simplify the handling of digital assets and transactions on the internet.

Trading Pairs: In cryptocurrency, the term "trading pairs" describes the asset pair being traded (typically one cryptocurrency for another), for example, the "trading pair" ETH/BTC. With ETH/BTC you can buy Ethereum with Bitcoin, or sell Ethereum for Bitcoin. Of course, fiat-based trading pairs can be found on cryptocurrency exchanges as well. For example, BTC/USD.

Utility Crypto: Utility crypto is cryptocurrencies that have a specific use or utility beyond being a form of payment or an investment asset. These cryptocurrencies are designed to provide a specific service or functionality within a blockchain network and are typically used to power decentralized applications (dApps) or to pay for transaction fees within a specific blockchain ecosystem. Examples of utility cryptocurrencies include Binance Coin and Basic Attention Token.

Wallet: A digital wallet is software that allows users to securely store, send, and receive cryptocurrencies. A wallet does not store the crypto itself but stores your private and public keys. The keys are used to interact with the blockchain network and manage your digital assets such as cryptocurrencies, tokens, and others.

Wallet Address: A wallet address in the realm of digital assets serves as a distinctive identifier, akin to a bank account number. This address is shared with individuals intending to transfer digital assets to you, with the transfer landing in your designated address. A wallet address consists of two elements: a public key and a private key. Maintaining the confidentiality of your private key is critical to safeguard your digital assets from unauthorized access or theft..

Wallet Types: Different kinds of wallets are employed to save and handle digital valuables like cryptocurrencies, tokens, and more. The primary ones are:

- *Hardware Wallets*: These are tangible devices that house your private keys in an offline mode, establishing them as one of the safest methods to keep your digital assets. Ledger Nano S, Trezor, Safepal, and KeepKey are some instances.

- *Software Wallets*: These are digital wallets that can be set up on your PC, smartphone, or tablet. Notable examples of such wallets include Guarda, Exodus, Coinbase Wallet, MetaMask, Trust Wallet, and Electrum

They can be further divided into:

- *Desktop Wallets*: Wallets installed on your computer, providing you with full control over your digital assets. Examples include Exodus, Electrum, and Atomic Wallet.

- *Mobile Wallets*: These are software wallets that can be installed on your mobile phone, providing you with the ability to manage your digital assets on the go. Examples include Trust Wallet, Mycelium, and Coinomi.

- *Web Wallets*: These are online wallets that can be accessed from any device with an internet connection. They are less secure than hardware and software wallets, but they are convenient to use. Examples include MyEtherWallet, MetaMask, and Coinbase Wallet.

- *Paper Wallets*: These are physical documents that contain your private keys in the form of a QR code or a string of characters. You may receive a paper wallet when visiting a Bitcoin ATM. However, as the wallet is just a piece of paper, it is highly susceptible to physical damage, which may hinder your ability to access your assets.

Whales: Crypto whales refer to individuals or organizations possessing substantial volumes of a particular digital currency. Broadly, a crypto whale is an entity that owns such a hefty amount of digital currency that they have the capacity to sway market values considerably through the trading of large quantities of coins and tokens.

World Reserve Currency: A currency that is widely accepted and held in significant quantities by governments and institutions around the world as a means of international trade, investment, and reserve holdings. The dominant world reserve currency is the U.S. dollar (USD), which is used as a standard for valuing other currencies and settling international transactions. The status of the USD as a world reserve currency has significant economic and geopolitical implications, but there are concerns about the potential risks and vulnerabilities of relying too heavily on a single currency for international trade and investment.

Managing Cookies: Take Control of Your Online Crumbs!

When you're browsing the internet, websites often leave little pieces of information called "cookies," on your computer. These cookies help websites remember things like what's in your shopping cart or if you're logged in. Sometimes, though, you might want to manage these cookies to protect your privacy or keep your browsing snappy.

For Folks Using Google Chrome: Google's Cookie Manager: Google has a handy guide that shows you how to control cookies right from your Chrome browser. You can decide if you want to allow cookies from some websites while blocking others, or if you want to clear all the cookies off your computer like shaking out a cookie jar.

See the resources page for Google Chrome instructions:

TamingCryptoBook.com/Resources

For Those Using Microsoft Edge: Microsoft's Cookie Commander: If you're using Microsoft Edge, check out Microsoft's guide to taking charge of your cookies. Just like organizing a real cookie jar, this guide helps you keep the cookies you want and toss out the ones you don't.

    Remember, managing cookies is about balancing convenience and privacy. Take control of your cookie settings to create a browsing experience that's just right for you!

- See the resources page for Microsoft Edge instructions:

    TamingCryptoBook.com/Resources

Questions to Consider When Selecting an Exchange

- **Jurisdiction**. Can you legally use the exchange where you live?
- **Ease of use**. How easy is it for a beginner to use the interface?
- **Liquidity levels**. How many users does the exchange have and how well-funded is it?
- **Asset choices**. Does it have the coins you are interested in buying and exchanging?
- **Security**. What type of security systems does the exchange have? What sort of wallets do they have connected to the exchange? Do they have a good reputation for dealing with unexpected hacks? Have they been hacked?
- **Reputation**. What is each exchange's reputation? It will be clear from research which exchanges rise above the rest and why.
- **Trading fees**. What are the trading or "gas" fees? Every exchange has its own fee schedule.
- **Customer support**. Is there support that's easy for you to use?
- **Insurance**. Does the exchange offer insurance against the unexpected, since these exchanges are not covered by the FDIC?
- **Tech infrastructure**. How easy and seamless are your transactions? Different exchanges use different technology.
- **Leverage and products**. Aside from buying a coin, are there other ways that you can make money and profit on this exchange? Are there staking or mining opportunities?
- **Deposit and withdrawal limits**. Are there minimum requirements to use the exchange? Do they have withdrawal limits? Often, withdrawal

limits differ depending on whether you trade anonymously or under your name.
- **Security holding period**. Do they have a holding period when you transfer fiat onto their exchange? If so, what is it?
- **Transparency**. Are fees easy to understand?
- **User experience**. Is using the exchange easy and enjoyable when you're using it?
- **Account verification**. How long is the account verification process, and what are the transfer and deposit processing times?

See resources page on the Taming Crypto Website: **tamingcryptobook.com/resources**

Take the Investor Type quiz: **tamingcryptobook.com/investor-type**

Acknowledgements

I was contemplating over a cup of hot tea what makes for a good book. I believe that it's a story that entertains and ideally, teaches us a new way to think. And what makes for a great book? A story that does all that, then ends before we're ready to say goodbye.

Taming Crypto is my humble attempt at writing such a book that engages the reader on a subject that has historically been a generally ominous topic, making it digestible and easy to move through while providing an initial plan for delving into digital assets for oneself.

If that's your experience, then mission accomplished! Of course, this venture took the support of a team.

The world is a better place thanks to people who develop and support the talents of others. I owe deep gratitude to the team of creatives that got Taming Crypto up and running. The editors and contributors were many: Torund Bryhn, Zachary Houghton, Richard Willett, Lisa Duncan, Heidi Stangeland, Ingvil Gaasland, Evangelina Chavez, Shana Pereira and Adam Russell. The artists who crafted the book cover and the interior images were also vital in setting the playful tone of the book. From bolstering the chapter structures to reimagining the journey of the FOMOs to include some poignant moments that emphasize critical lessons for you as a crypto newbie, the finished product would not be as rich without the combined efforts of everyone involved.

To my family and friends who showed much patience with my absence as I sat in my kitchen writing the book, and to those who allowed me to use these crazy metaphors to teach them what I had learned and done,

I thank you for fueling me to complete Taming Crypto. Your encouragement kept me going.

Lastly, I want to thank Divine Inspiration, the creative spark that lives inside of me. Because of Source, every day is another adventure giving me new frontiers to venture into!